ALevelPhysicsOnline.com

ACKNOWLEDGEMENTS

This series of books has been a pretty big undertaking!

I'm extremely grateful to the following contributors who have helped write many of the questions in this guide. Between them, they have many years of experience as Heads of Physics, Heads or Science or Outreach Officers promoting STEM subjects.

- Dr Peter Edmunds
- Muhammad Kashif Jamal
- Dr Dan Jones
- Dave Grainger
- Matthew Lewis
- Melissa Lord

Joe Cattermole (a recent Physics Graduate) collated the first draft and wrote hundreds of additional questions before James Hills and Rufus Jones assisted with formatting and proofreading the many edits that I made.

It was a real team effort and I hope the resulting book will be useful to you as you study A Level Physics.

Lewis Matheson

HOW TO USE THIS BOOK

The idea is pretty simple – attempt a few questions everyday to help build upon your existing knowledge and strengthen understanding as you commence your A Level Physics course.

To find out a little bit more about how to use this book scan the QR code, or go to the webpage below, to watch a video explaining everything you need to know.

ALevelPhysicsOnline.com/**book-1**

Symbols to learn

- Proportional

DATA AND FORMULAE

Add useful information to this page as you're working through the book.

Resistors in Parallel

$$\frac{1}{R_T} = \frac{1}{R_1} + \frac{1}{R_2} + \ldots$$

$g = 9.81\ N\,kg^{-1}$

$m_{electron} = 9.11 \times 10^{-31}\ kg$

JULY

JULY

In July we're going to start covering some of the basics – a lot of which you will already have covered in your GCSE Science course and GCSE Maths.

This includes:

- Pythagoras and trigonometry with right-angled triangles
- Standard form
- Significant figures
- Rearranging formulas
- Simple calculations (based on your GCSE knowledge)

Many of the questions will be quick and straightforward, others may appear a little more tricky, but it's worth persevering. A Level Physics relies a lot more on mathematics than GCSE Physics - so you must be familiar with the techniques you practise this month.

There are answers in the back of the book for you to mark your work. For full worked solutions please visit the A Level Physics website.

Worked Examples

1. Calculate the **area**, in m^2, of a circle with a radius of:

   a. 1.25 m $A = \pi r^2 = \pi \times 1.25^2 = 4.91\ m^2$ (3 sf)

   b. 12.5 mm $A = \pi r^2 = \pi \times (12.5 \times 10^{-3})^2 = 4.91 \times 10^{-4}\ m^2$ (3 sf)

   c. 125 μm $A = \pi r^2 = \pi \times (125 \times 10^{-6})^2 = 4.91 \times 10^{-8}\ m^2$ (Standard form)

2. Calculate the **mass** of a robin flying at 8.9 m s^{-1} when it has a kinetic energy of 879 mJ.

$$E_k = \frac{1}{2} m v^2 \qquad m = \frac{2E_k}{v^2} = \frac{2 \times 879 \times 10^{-3}}{8.9^2}$$

Equation + Rearrange; 2 sf; Working out

$$m = 0.02219$$

$$m = 2.2 \times 10^{-2}\ kg$$

2 sf; Units

3. Calculate the **horizontal component** of a force of 9.7 N acting at 17° above the horizontal.

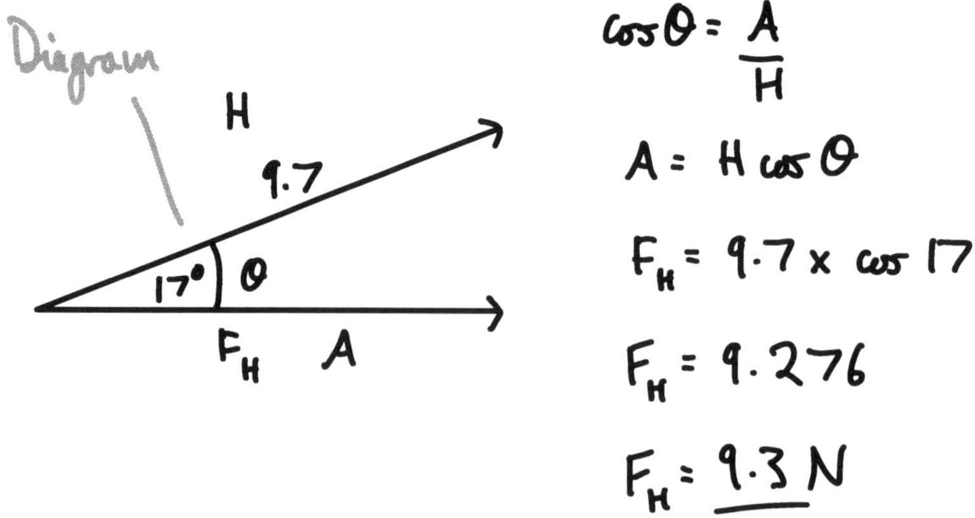

$$\cos\theta = \frac{A}{H}$$

$$A = H\cos\theta$$

$$F_H = 9.7 \times \cos 17$$

$$F_H = 9.276$$

$$F_H = 9.3\ N$$

1st July

1 2 3

1. Calculate the **angle**, θ, in the triangle with a hypotenuse of length 10.0 cm and an opposite side length of 8.00 cm.

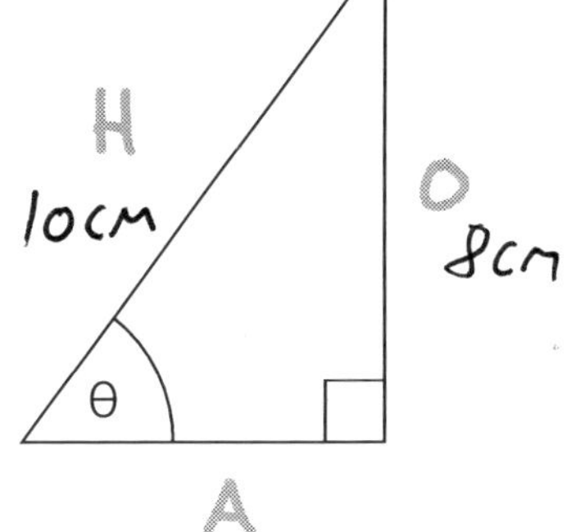

$\sin\theta = \frac{op}{h}$

$\sin\theta = \frac{8}{10}$ $\theta = \sin^{-1}\left(\frac{4}{5}\right)$

$\theta = 53.1^\circ$

2. Write down the **proportionality relationship** between kinetic energy and (non-relativistic) mass for a moving object.

$E_K = \frac{1}{2}mv^2$

$E_k \propto M$ $E_k \propto M$

$E_k \propto M$ $E_k \propto M$

$E_k \propto M$ $E_k \propto M$

3. Calculate the **kinetic energy** and **momentum** of a car with a mass of 1200 kg and a velocity of 30 m s^{-1}.

m = 1200 kg v = 30 m s^{-1} $p = mv$ $E_K = \frac{1}{2}mv^2$

$E_k = \frac{1}{2}MV^2$

$= \frac{1}{2}(1200)(30)^2$

$E_k = 5.4 \times 10^5$ J

$P = MV$

$= (1200)(30)$

$= 3.6 \times 10^4$ kgms^{-1}

2nd July

1 2 3

1. Calculate the length of the **hypotenuse** in this triangle with an angle of 40° and an adjacent side length of 2.8 m.

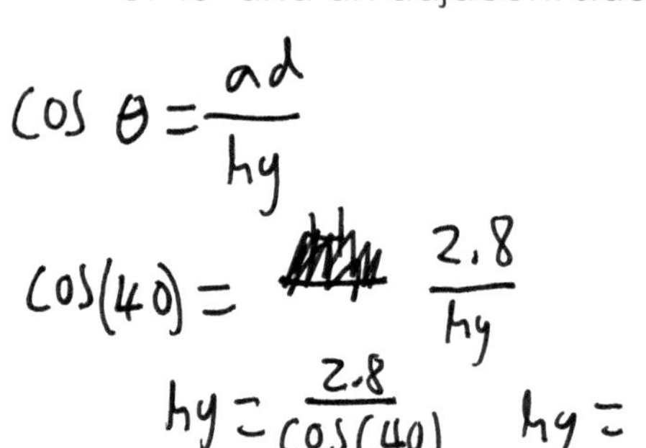

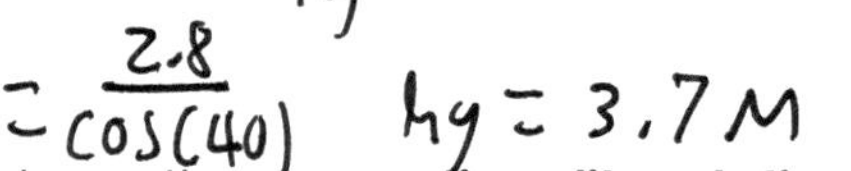

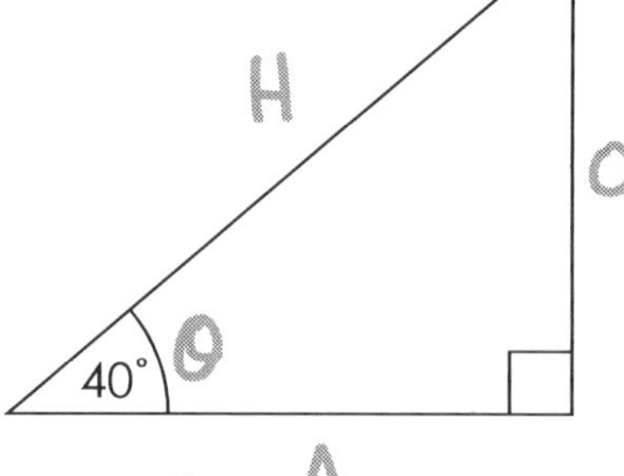

2. Write down the **proportionality relationship** between resultant force and acceleration.

$F \propto a$ $F = ma$ $\therefore F \propto a$

$F \propto a$ $F = ma$

$F \propto a$ $\therefore F \propto a$

$F \propto a$

$F \propto a$

3. Explain what a **vector** quantity is and identify which of these quantities are vectors:

S V V S S V
Speed, velocity, force, mass, energy and weight

A Vector has both magnitude and direction

3rd July

1. State **Pythagoras'** Theorem.

$a^2 + b^2 = c^2$

where c is the hypotenuse of a right angled triangle and a and b are the two shortest sides.

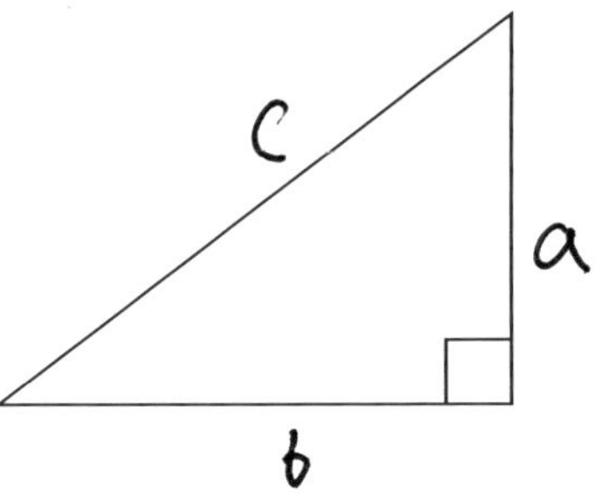

2. Write down the **proportionality relationship** between and frequency and time period for a wave.

$f = \frac{1}{t}$

$\therefore f \propto \frac{1}{T}$

$\therefore f \propto \frac{1}{T}$

3. Calculate the **frequency** of a sound wave that has a velocity of 330 m s^{-1} and a wavelength of 2.60 m.

$v = f\lambda$

$330 = f \times 2.6$

$f = \frac{330}{2.6}$

$f = 127\ Hz$

4th July

1. Calculate the length of the **hypotenuse** of an orthogonal triangle with sides of length 3.3 cm and 4.0 cm.

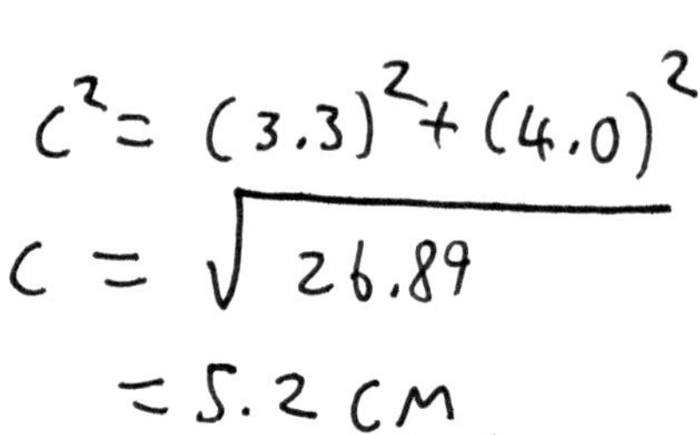

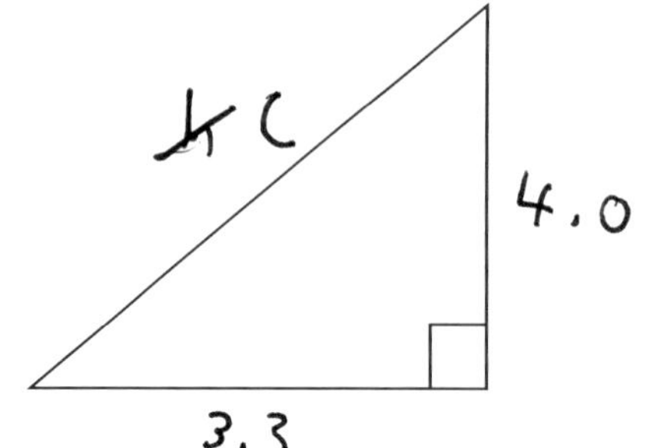

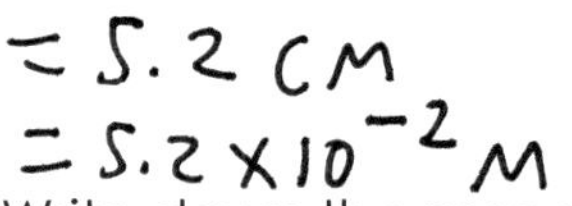

2. Write down the **proportionality relationship** between acceleration and mass, for a constant net force.

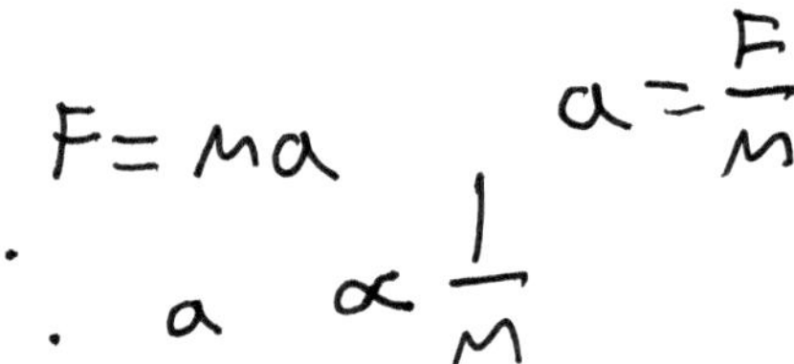

3. Calculate the **current** in a circuit if 50 C of charge is transferred in 20 s.

$Q = It$

$50 = I \times 20$

$I = \frac{50}{20}$

$I = 2.5$ A

5th July

1 2 3

1. Calculate the length of the **side** of a right-angled triangle if the hypotenuse is 10 m and the other side is 7.0 cm.

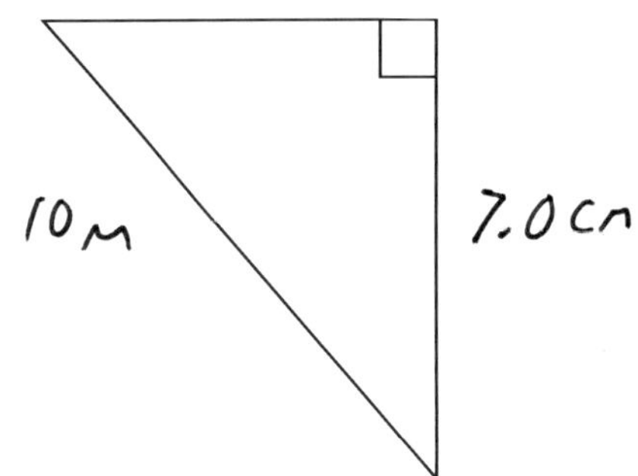

$a^2+b^2=c^2$

$7^2+b^2=10^2$

$b=\sqrt{(100-49)}$

$=\sqrt{51}$

$b=7.1$ cm

2. Write down the **proportionality relationship** between momentum and velocity.

$p=mv$

$p \propto v$

$p \propto v$

$p \propto v$

$p \propto v$

3. Describe, in as much detail as you can, the structure of an **atom**.

- mostly empty space
- positive nucleus containing neutrons and protons
- negative electrons in orbitals

6th July

1 2 3

1. Calculate the length of a **side** of a right-angled triangle if the hypotenuse is 42 m and the other side is 40 m.

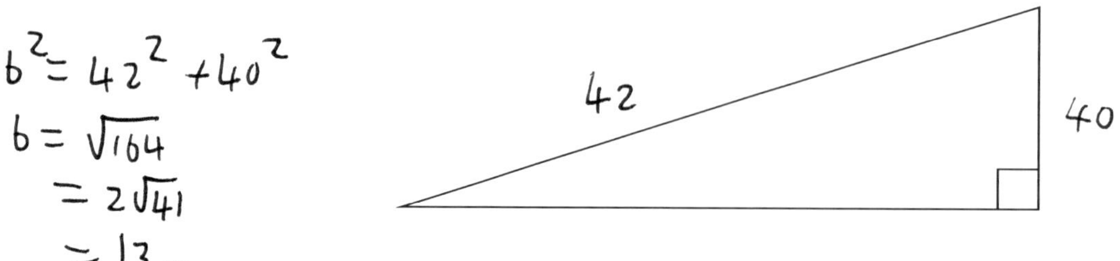

2. Write down the **proportionality relationship** between kinetic energy and velocity.

$ke = \frac{1}{2} m v^2$

$\therefore$ ke ∝ V E_k ∝ V

ke ∝ V E_k ∝ V

ke E_k ∝ V

E_k ∝ V E_k ∝ V

3. Describe, in a **DC circuit**, what electric current is and how **conventional current** is defined.

+ → −

7th July

1 2 3

1. Write the following numbers in **standard form**:
   a. 8 990 000 000
   b. 299 790 000
   c. 96 485

2. For the following **triangle** where O = 10.00, H = 14.14 and θ = 45.0˚ calculate to 3 sf:
   a. The ratio of side O to H
   b. sinθ
   c. The ratio of side A to H
   d. cosθ

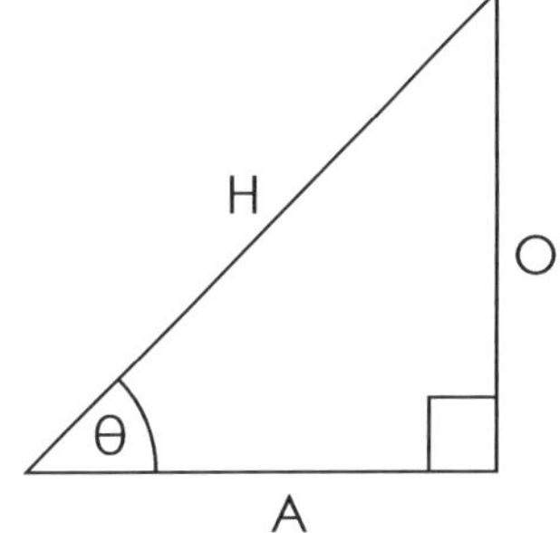

3. Calculate the **distance** travelled by an object that has a speed of 16 m s^{-1} in exactly one minute.

8th July

1 2 3

1. Write the following numbers in **standard form**:
   a. 0.002 898
   b. 0.000 000 000 000 000 000 000 000 000 000 910 94
   c. 0.000 000 056 70

2. For the following **triangle** where O = 2.20, H = 4.40 and θ = 30.0˚ calculate to 3 sf:
   a. The ratio of side O to H
   b. sinθ
   c. The ratio of side A to H
   d. cosθ

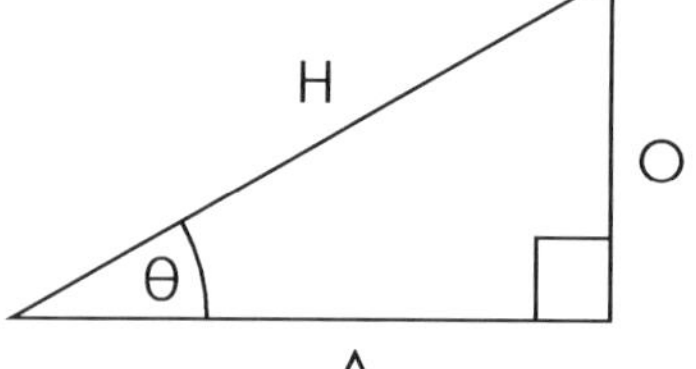

3. Calculate the **speed of light** if red light has a frequency 4.3×10^{14} Hz and a wavelength of 7.0×10^{-7} m.

9th July

1 2 3

1. Write down the charge, in **coulombs**, of:
   a. An electron
   b. A neutron
   c. A proton

2. Rearrange $v = u + at$ to make ***u*** the subject.

3. Calculate the **average acceleration** of a runner who starts at rest and reaches a velocity of 6.00 m s^{-1} in 9.00 s.

10th July

1 2 3

1. Calculate, **without** using a calculator:
   a. 2.0×10^4 multiplied by 4.0×10^7
   b. 4.0×10^4 multiplied by 2.0×10^7
   c. 3.0×10^4 multiplied by 3.0×10^7
   d. 3.0×10^4 multiplied by 4.0×10^7

2. Rearrange $v^2 = u^2 + 2as$ to make ***u*** the subject.

3. Calculate the **final** velocity of a rocket if it starts at rest and uniformly accelerates at 0.80 m s^{-2} over 20 km.

11th July

1 2 3

1. Calculate, **without** using a calculator:
   a. 4.0×10^4 divided by 2.0×10^7
   b. 2.0×10^4 divided by 4.0×10^7
   c. 2.0×10^7 divided by 4.0×10^7
   d. 2.0×10^7 divided by 4.0×10^4

2. Rearrange the following to make **d** the subject:
   a. $E = V / d$

   b. $n\lambda = d\sin\theta$

   c. $A = \pi d^2 / 4$

3. Calculate the **acceleration** of an object that slows down from 70 m s^{-1} to rest in 5.0 minutes.

12th July

1 2 3

1. Calculate, **without** a calculator:
   a. 2.0×10^4 plus 4.0×10^4
   b. 2.0×10^5 plus 4.0×10^4
   c. 2.0×10^4 plus 4.0×10^5
   d. 8.0×10^4 plus 4.0×10^5

2. Rearrange *the following* to make **Q** the subject.
   a. $r = p / BQ$
   b. $V = W / Q$
   c. $F = BQv$

3. A wave travels at 5.00×10^4 m s^{-1}. Calculate its **wavelength** if its frequency is 7.00×10^2 Hz.

13th July

1 2 3

1. Calculate, **without** a calculator:
   a. 2.0×10^4 minus 4.0×10^4
   b. 2.0×10^5 minus 4.0×10^4
   c. 2.0×10^4 minus 4.0×10^5
   d. 8.0×10^4 minus 4.0×10^5

2. State **Newton's 1st Law** and provide a real-life example.

3. Complete the tip-to-tail vector diagram by drawing in the resultant vector, working out its **magnitude** and measuring the **angle** from the vertical.

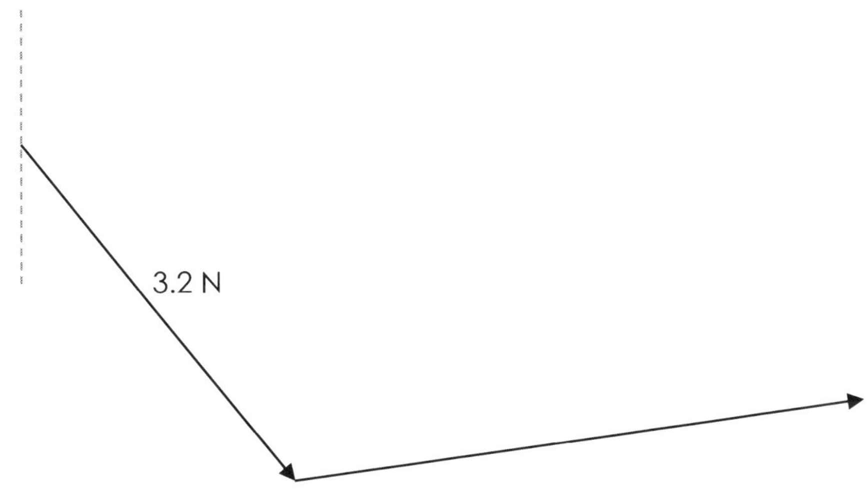

14th July

1 2 3

1. Calculate the **mean**, **mode** and **median** of the following set of numbers:

   2, 3, 3, 3, 6, 8, 10

2. State **Newton's 2nd Law** and describe a real-life example to illustrate it in action.

3. Complete the vector diagram using the **parallelogram** method. Draw in the resultant vector and work out its magnitude.

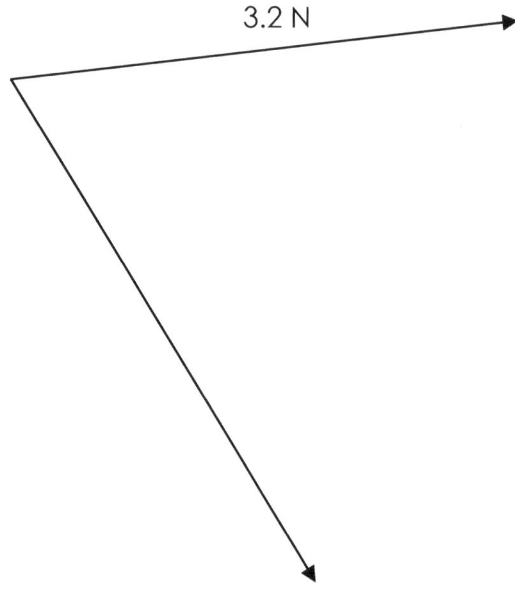

15th July

1 2 3

1. Calculate the **mean**, **mode** and **median** of the following set of numbers:

   45, 46, 39, 40, 50, 45, 51

2. State **Newton's 3rd Law** (between two objects A and B) and give a relevant example.

3. Calculate, using a **graphical** method, the size of the resultant force produced by these two perpendicular forces (where 1 cm = 1 N).

16th July

1 2 3

1. Write the following numbers in **standard form** to **3 significant** figures.
   a. 0.000 000 000 000 000 000 000 000 000 000 000 662 607
   b. 0.000 000 000 000 000 000 000 000 001 660 539
   c. 0.000 000 000 008 854 188

2. A car is travelling at a constant velocity of 30 m s^{-1}. Describe the **forces** acting on it and draw a diagram to illustrate your answer.

3. Calculate, using a **mathematical** method, the size of the resultant force produced by these two perpendicular forces and the angle through which it acts.

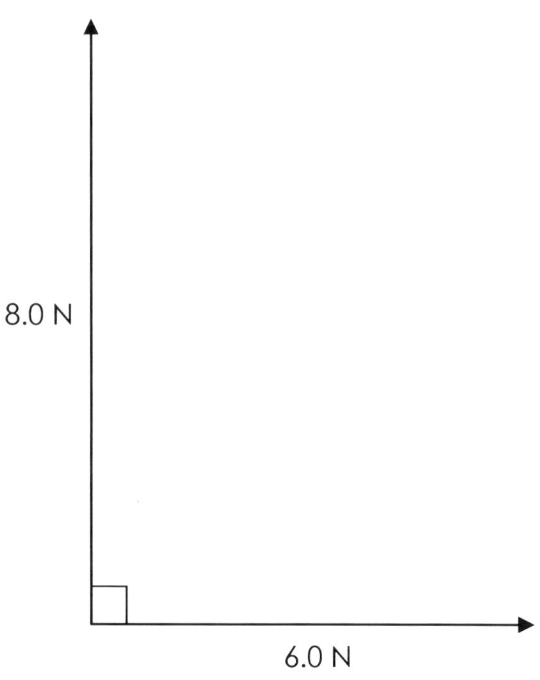

17th July

1 2 3

1. Write the following numbers in **standard form** to **3 significant** figures.
   a. 0.000 000 000 000 000 000 000 000 001 672 622
   b. 0.000 000 000 000 000 000 000 000 001 674 927
   c. 0.000 000 000 000 000 000 000 013 806
   d. 0.000 000 000 066 743

2. State the relative **masses**, relative **charges** and **ionisation** power of alpha, beta minus and gamma radiation.

3. Calculate the size and angle of the resultant force, using **scale drawing**, produced by a downwards vertical force of 40 N and a horizontal force to the right of 60 N.

18th July

1 2 3

1. Calculate the following to an **appropriate** number of significant figures:
   a. 32.1 x 49
   b. 32 x 49
   c. 32.1 x 48.9
   d. 32 x 48.927

2. Calculate the **velocity** of a 600 g basketball ball when it has 67.5 J of kinetic energy.

3. Calculate the size of the resultant force, using a **mathematical** method, produced by a vertical force of 950 N down and a horizontal force of 390 N to the left.

19th July

1 2 3

1. Calculate the following to an **appropriate** number of significant figures:
   a. 30 + 50
   b. 30.1 ÷ 49.97
   c. 30.0 + 50.0
   d. 30 x 49.97

2. Calculate the **opposite** and **adjacent** sides of the triangle if F = 550 N and θ = 39°.

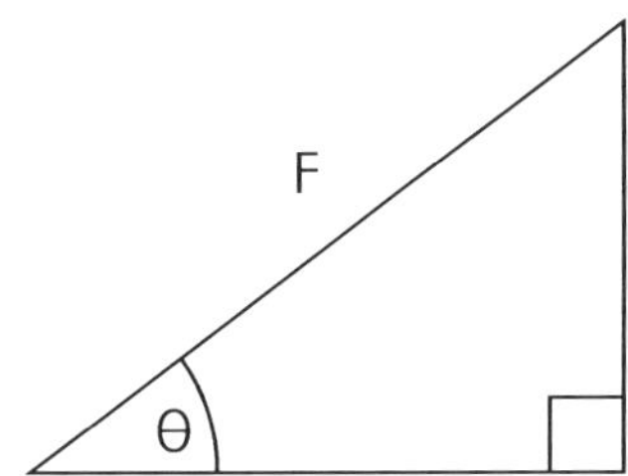

3. Describe the changes to a nucleus's **proton** and **mass** numbers if it decays by emitting:
   a. Alpha radiation

   b. Beta minus radiation

   c. Gamma radiation

20th July

1 2 3

1. Calculate the following to an **appropriate** number of significant figures:
    a. 9.2×10^{2} multiplied by 8.3×10^{-2}
    b. 9.21×10^{2} multiplied by 8.3×10^{-2}
    c. 9.2×10^{22} multiplied by 8.317×10^{-20}
    d. 9.210×10^{22} multiplied by 8.317×10^{-20}

2. Calculate the **horizontal** and **vertical** components of a resultant force of 100 N acting at 30˚ above the horizontal.

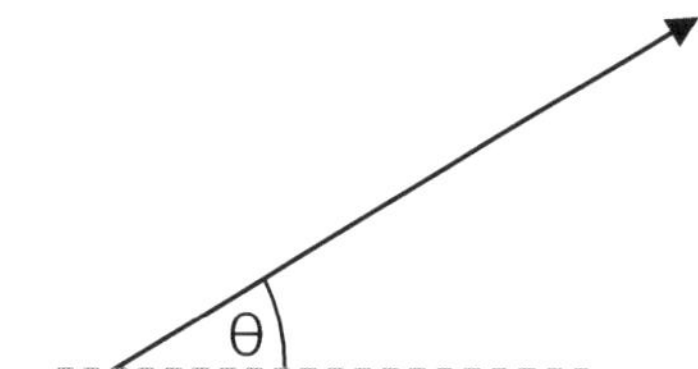

3. Calculate the **initial** velocity of a ball if its final velocity is 3.00 m s^{-1} after it accelerates at 24 m s^{-2} over 0.15 m.

21st July

1. Solve:
   a. $4x + 20 = 0$
   b. $15x - 30 > 0$
   c. $8x - 16 < 0$
   d. $x^2 - 4 = 0$

2. Calculate the **horizontal** and **vertical** components of a force of 24.0 kN acting at 19° from the vertical plane.

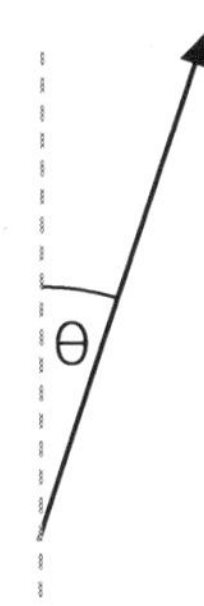

3. Calculate the **maximum** theoretical height a 300 g ball would reach if fired vertically upwards with an initial kinetic energy of 400 J.

   Assume negligible air resistance and use $g = 9.81 \text{ N kg}^{-1}$

22nd July

1 2 3

1. Define the **joule**.

2. Describe what the **area** underneath a velocity-time graph represents.

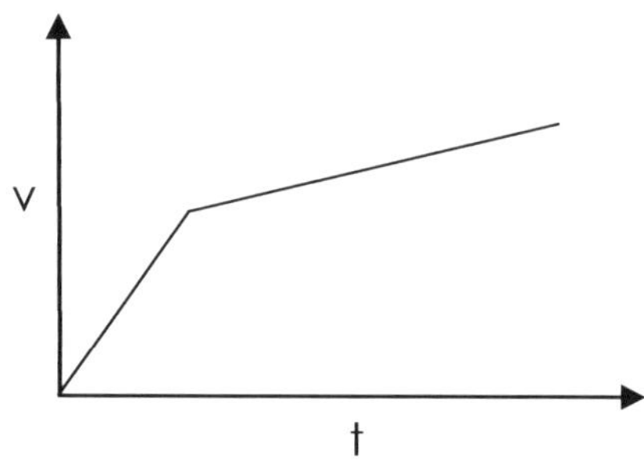

3. Calculate the **energy transferred per second** in a resistor with 2.0 V across it and 0.30 A through it.

23rd July

1 2 3

1. Define the **frequency** of a wave.

2. Calculate the **area** under the graph of y = 3 between x = 0 and x = 3.

   Sketching the graph may help.

3. Calculate the **total resistance** when a 1.0 kΩ resistor is connected in series to two 400 Ω resistors.

24th July

1 2 3

1. Define **fission** and **fusion**.

2. Calculate the **area** under the graph of y = 2x between x = 0 and x = 4.

   Sketching the graph may help.

3. Calculate the **frequency** of a sound wave with a speed of 330 m s^{-1} and a wavelength of 30 cm.

25th July

1 2 3

1. $y = mx + c$ describes a graph with a straight line of gradient 'm' and y-intercept 'c'.

   Write down the **gradient** and **y-intercept** of the graphs with equation:

   a. $y = 2x + 3$

   b. $y = 3x + 2$

   c. $y = 6x + 3$

   d. $y = 6 + 3x$

2. Rearrange $F = BIL\sin\theta$ to make:

   a. **B** the subject

   b. **I** the subject

   c. **L** the subject

   d. **θ** the subject

3. Write down the number of **protons**, **neutrons** and **electrons** in the following atoms:

$^{56}_{26}Fe$ $^{54}_{26}Fe$ $^{59}_{27}Co$ $^{60}_{28}Ni$

26th July

1 2 3

1. Write down the **gradient** and **y-intercept** of the graphs with equation:
   a. $y = 3x + 5$
   b. $2y = 4x + 2$
   c. $x + 3 = y$
   d. $y - 4 = x / 2$

2. Rearrange $g = Gm / r^2$ to make **r** the subject.

3. Calculate the **acceleration** of a 1825 N boat when there is a thrust of 350 N from the engines and total drag forces of 185 N.

27th July

1 2 3

1. Calculate the **gradient** and **y-intercept** of the line with equation:
   a. $2y = 4x + 8$
   b. $4y - 6 = x/2$
   c. $0 = x + y$
   d. $x = 0.5y + 2$

2. Rearrange $V_g = Gm / r$ to make **m** the subject.

3. A ray of light at 25° to the surface of a plane mirror is reflected (with a specular reflection). Calculate the angle of **reflection** (a diagram will help).

28th July

1. Calculate the gradient and hence the **equation** of the straight-line graph that goes through the points (1, 2) and (5, 10).

2. Rearrange the following to make **p** the subject:

   a. $m = p / v$

   b. $pV = NkT$

   c. $E_k = p^2 / 2m$

3. Sketch the arrangement of particles in a **solid**, a **liquid** and a **gas**.

29th July

1 2 3

1. Calculate the **equation** of the straight-line graph that goes through the point (1, 2) and has a gradient of 3.

2. Use the symbol '≈' to describe the **small-angle approximation** involving sin θ, cos θ and tan θ.

3. A 2.1 kg wheel rolls down a slope, losing 0.62 kJ of gravitational potential energy.

   Calculate the **height** it rolls down.

30th July

1 2 3

1. **Sketch** the graphs of $y = 3x + 1$ and $y = x + 3$.

2. Write down **two** ways of defining radioactive **half-life**.

3. Calculate the **acceleration** of a car when it slows down from 10 m s^{-1} to 3.0 m s^{-1} in 2.5 s.

31st July

1 2 3

1. **Sketch** the graphs of $y = e^x$ and $y = e^{-x}$.

2. Define electrical **resistance**.

3. Complete the following **nuclear** equations:

$$^{238}_{92}U \rightarrow Th + He$$

$$^{234}Th \rightarrow Pa + {}_{-1}\beta$$

$$^{234}Pa \rightarrow \quad + {}_{-1}\beta$$

JULY REVIEW

Record your progress at the end of the month and have another go at any questions you may have missed.

A Level Physics Content	Red	Amber	Green
I can use **standard form**.			
I can give an answer to an appropriate number of **significant figures**.			
I can use **Pythagoras** to calculate the length of the third side of a triangle.			
I can identify the **opposite**, **adjacent** and **hypotenuse** of a right-angled triangle.			
I can resolve the **horizontal** and **vertical** components of a vector quantity.			
I can **rearrange** simple equations.			
I can recall **Newton's 3 Laws**.			

Any other comments:

AUGUST

AUGUST

It's the middle of the summer holidays and you're making great progress so far!

A lot of the questions are still based on your GCSE knowledge but these skills are essential for every single topic next year.

You will probably have many questions about the structure of your forthcoming A Level course, so I have put some resources together for you to have a look at.

This includes:

- An overview of A Level Physics
- Introductory videos for every topic
- Links to GCSE videos if you need a quick recap

ALevelPhysicsOnline.com/**introduction-to-a-level-physics**

1st August

1 2 3

1. Calculate the **area**, in m^2, of a circle with a radius of:
   a. 2.0 m
   b. 4.0 m
   c. 4.0 cm
   d. 4.0 mm

2. Complete the tip-to-tail vector diagram by drawing in the resultant vector, working out its **magnitude** and measuring the **angle** from the vertical.

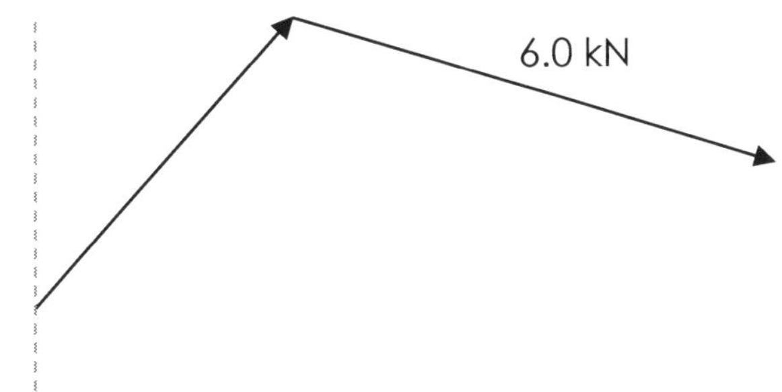

3. Write down the seven **base units** that all other derived units can be expressed in.

▪

▪

▪

▪

▪

▪

▪

2nd August

1 2 3

1. Calculate the **area**, in m², of a circle with:
   a. Radius 5.0 mm
   b. Diameter 5.0 mm
   c. Diameter 10.0 mm
   d. Circumference 10.0 mm

2. Find out what the following **symbols** in A Level Physics represent:
   a. G
   b. ε_0
   c. pc
   d. h
   e. eV
   f. m_e

3. Show that the base units for **joules** are kg m^2 s^{-2}.

3rd August

1 2 3

1. Calculate the **area**, in m^2, of a triangle with a:
   a. Vertical height of 36 cm and a base of 11 cm
   b. Vertical height of 18 cm and a base of 36 cm
   c. Vertical height of 36.2 cm and a base of 1.13 m

2. Complete the tip-to-tail vector diagram by drawing in the resultant vector, working out its **magnitude** and measuring the **angle** from the vertical.

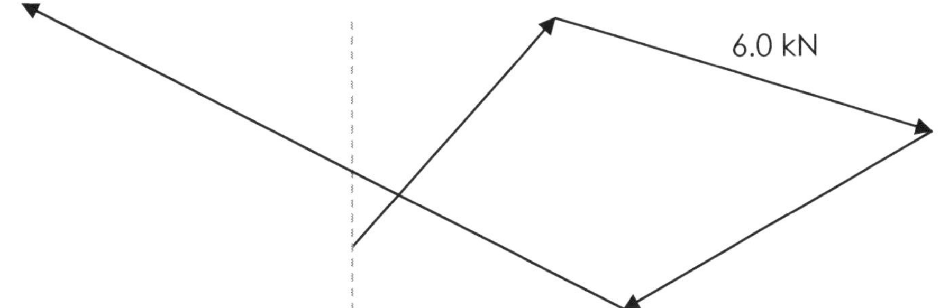

3. Calculate the **horizontal** and **vertical** components of a 10.1 N force acting at 17.2° above the horizontal.

4th August

1 2 3

1. Calculate the **surface area**, in m^2, of a sphere with a radius of:
    a. 0.80 m
    b. 0.40 m
    c. 0.20 m
    d. 0.10 m

2. Find out the values for the following **constants** used regularly throughout A Level Physics:
    a. Mass of an electron
    b. Planck's constant
    c. Speed of light
    d. Elementary charge
    e. Gravitational field strength on Earth's surface
    f. Acceleration due to gravity on Earth

3. Calculate the **direction** of the resultant force when 9.81 N acts to the right and 3.24 N acts downwards.

5th August

1 2 3

1. Calculate the **volume**, in m^3, of a sphere with a radius of:
   a. 0.80 m
   b. 0.40 m
   c. 0.20 m
   d. 0.10 m

2. Write down the **proportionality relationship** between gravitational potential energy and mass (for a uniform field).

3. Calculate the **combined** resistance of a 30 Ω and 50 Ω resistor connected in parallel.

6th August

1 2 3

1. Calculate the **volume** and **surface area** of a cylinder with a radius of 92 mm and a length of 2.7 m.

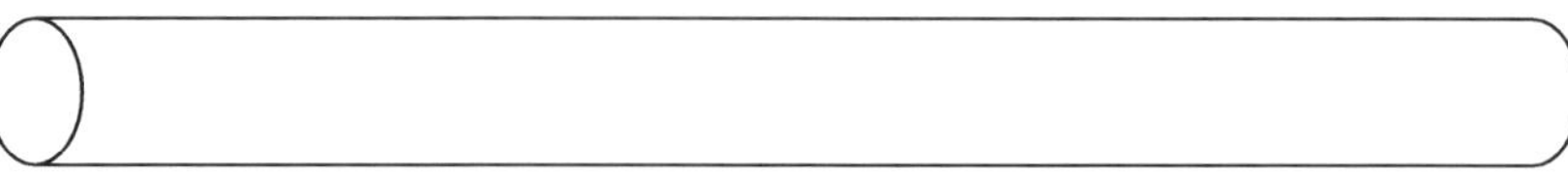

2. Trace the following **curves**.

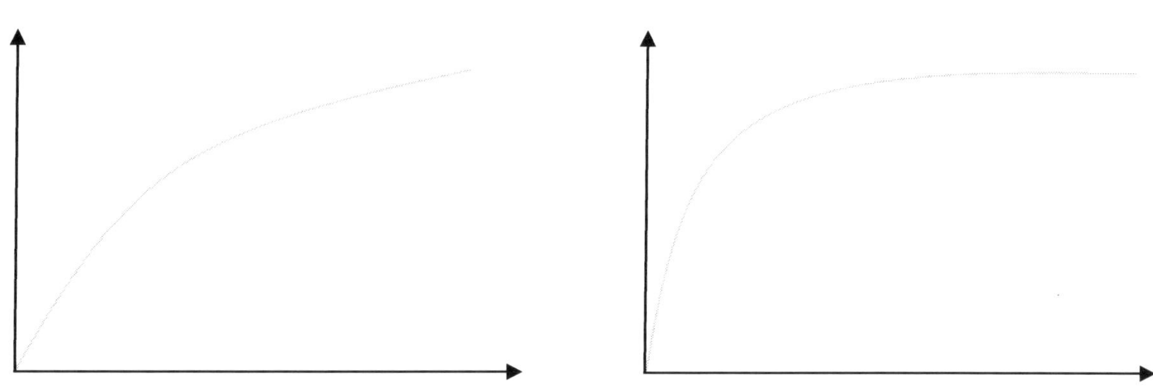

3. A catapult launches a stone vertically at 25 m s^{-1}. By equating kinetic energy and gravitational potential energy, calculate the **maximum height** reached.

   Assume there are no energy losses and there is negligible air resistance.

7th August

1 2 3

1. Calculate the **volume**, in m^3, and **surface area**, in m^2, of a sphere with a radius of:
   a. 82 mm
   b. 6.4 cm
   c. 6400 km
   d. 6.96×10^5 km

2. Rearrange the following to make **T** the subject:
   a. $f = 1 / T$
   b. $W = T\theta$
   c. $pV = nRT$
   d. $P = \sigma A T^4$

3. Calculate the **speed** of a wave that has a time period of 4.0 s and a wavelength of 40 m.

8th August

1 2 3

1. Calculate the **diameter**, in m, of a wire with a cross-sectional area of:
   a. $1.0\ m^2$
   b. $0.16\ m^2$
   c. $100\ mm^2$
   d. $1.7 \times 10^{-3}\ m^2$

2. Rearrange the following to make **ω** the subject:
   a. $P = T\omega$
   b. $v_{max} = \omega a$
   c. $F = m\omega^2 r$
   d. $E_k = \frac{1}{2}I\omega^2$

3. A radioactive sample has an initial activity of 2 000 Bq.

   Calculate the **activity** of the sample after 4 half-lives.

9th August

1 2 3

1. Calculate the **volume**, in m^3, of a cylinder with a :
   a. Radius of 920 mm and a height of 2.7 m
   b. Length of 20 m and diameter 1.9 mm
   c. Length 2.1 m and radius 0.89 mm

2. Rearrange the following to make **V** the subject:
   a. $\rho = m / V$
   b. $R = V / I$
   c. $pV = NkT$
   d. $P = V^2 / R$

3. 0.050 m^3 of a gas is at a pressure of 220 kPa. The volume is decreased to 0.010 m^3.

   Calculate the **pressure** of the gas after it has been compressed, provided the temperature has remained constant.

10th August

1 2 3

1. Calculate the gradient and hence the **equation** of the straight-line graph that goes through the points (0, 2) and (5, 7).

2. Rearrange the following to make **v** the subject:

   a. $P = Fv$

   b. $F = BQv$

   c. $F = mv^2 / r$

   d. $\Delta f / f = v / c$

3. The driving force of a motorbike's engine is 2 000 N and the resistive force the bike experiences is 600 N. The bike and rider have a total weight of 2800 N.

   Calculate the **acceleration**. Use $g = 9.81\ N\ kg^{-1}$.

11th August

1 2 3

1. Calculate the gradient and hence the **equation** of the straight-line graph that goes through the points (8, 11) and (-3, -22).

2. Rearrange the following to make **r** the subject:

   a. $T = Fr$

   b. $F = 6\pi\eta rv$

   c. $F = m\omega^2 r$

   d. $a = v^2 / r$

3. A mountain biker accelerates for 20 s from rest over a distance of 85 m. The cyclist and their bike have a mass of 110 kg.

   Calculate the **kinetic energy** gained by the cyclist.

12th August

1 2 3

1. Calculate the **equation** of the straight-line graph that goes through the point (9, 3) and has a gradient of -2.

2. **Describe**, in a practical investigation, what is meant by:
   a. An independent variable
   b. A dependent variable
   c. A control variable

3. Red light has a wavelength of approximately 700 nm, whereas violet light has a wavelength of approximately 400 nm.

   Calculate the **range** of **frequencies** of visible light.

13th August

1 2 3

1. Calculate the **area**, in m^2, of a circle with a diameter of:

   a. 0.800 mm

   b. 0.00142 m

   c. 805 μm

   d. 0.10 cm

2. Identify the **sinusoidal** curves below and trace the lines.

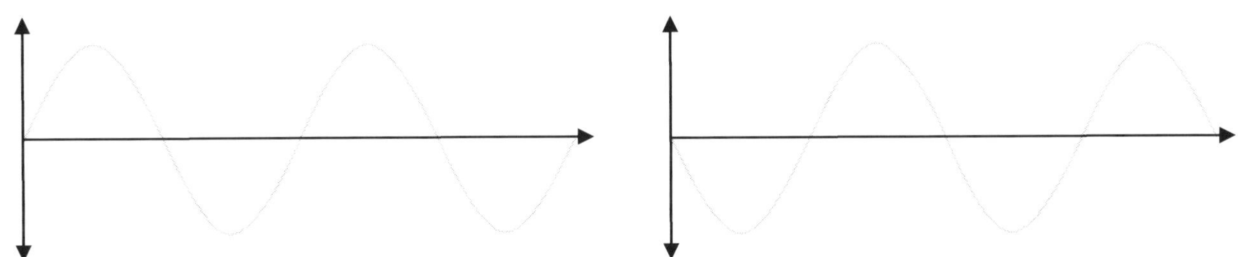

3. Two resistors are connected in series. The circuit is set up with a 6.0 V battery and has a current of 0.30 A. The first resistor has a resistance of 12 Ω.

   Calculate the **resistance** of the second resistor and the **potential difference** across each of the two resistors.

14th August

1 2 3

1. Sketch the **sinusoidal** curves with the same frequency and half the amplitude.

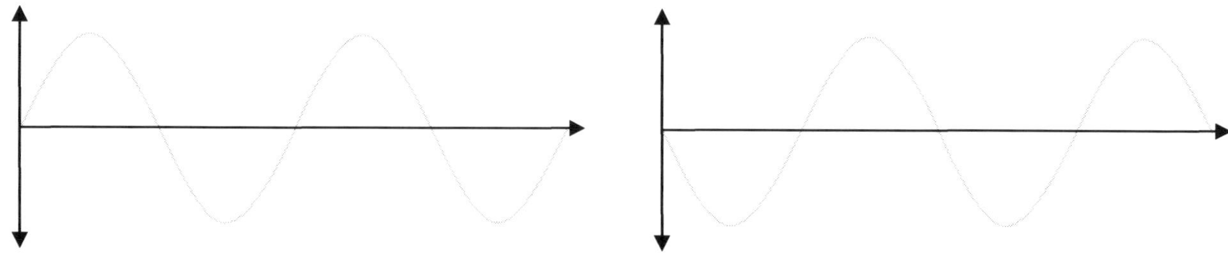

2. Sketch the **sinusoidal** curves with the same amplitude and twice the frequency.

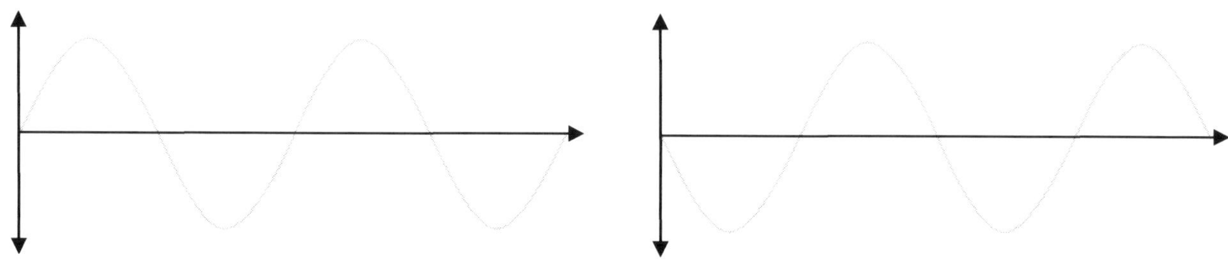

3. The half-life of a sample is 3.0 hours and the number of nuclei in the sample is 6.4×10^{10}.

   Calculate the **number** of original nuclei left after 1 day.

15th August

1 2 3

1. Sketch the **sinusoidal** curves with four times the frequency and half the amplitude.

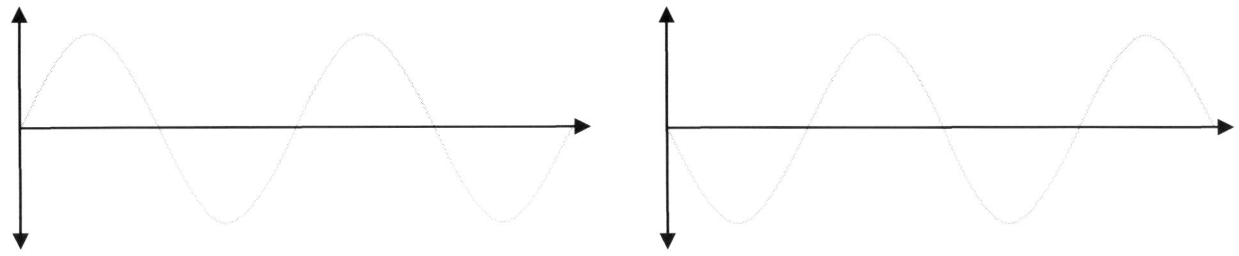

2. Find the **value** and **units** for the following constants:

    a. Avogadro's constant

    b. Molar gas constant

    c. Gravitational constant

    d. Elementary charge

3. The pressure of 22.4 cm^3 of a gas at 130˚C is 400 kPa. The pressure is gradually increased to 550 kPa.

    Calculate the **volume**, in m^3, of the gas after it has been compressed, provided the temperature remains constant.

16th August

1 2 3

1. Use one of the following symbols; <, <<, > or >>, to describe the **relationship** between:
   a. 10 and 9
   b. 100 and 9
   c. 3.7 and 4.1
   d. 660×10^{-9} and 6.5×10^{-7}

2. Rearrange the following to make $\boldsymbol{\omega_1}$ the subject:
   a. $\omega_2 = \omega_1 + at$
   b. $\omega_2^2 = \omega_1^2 + 2a\theta$
   c. $\theta = \omega_1 t + \frac{1}{2}at^2$
   d. $\theta = \frac{1}{2}(\omega_1 + \omega_2)t$

3. Use the expression for force, F = ke, and the area under a force-extension graph to **derive** an expression for elastic potential energy in terms of spring constant and extension.

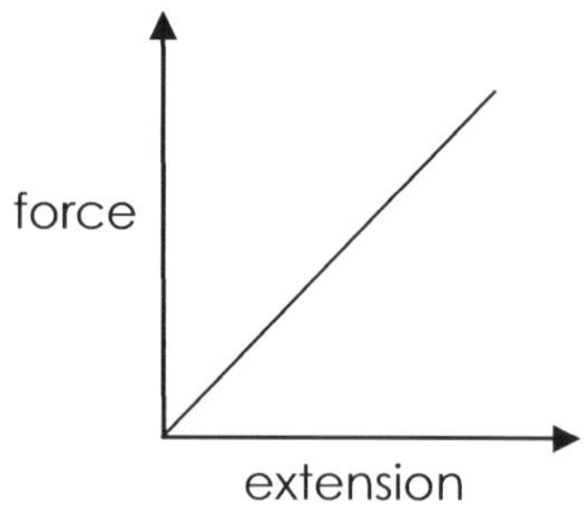

17th August

1 2 3

1. Use one of the following symbols; <, <<, > or >>, to describe the **relationship** between:
   a. 5.97×10^{24} and 4.87×10^{24}
   b. 5.97×10^{24} and 1.99×10^{30}
   c. 5.97×10^{24} and 6 000 000 000 000 000 000 000 000 000 000
   d. The mass of an electron and 1×10^{-30}

2. Rearrange the following to make **λ** the subject:
   a. $v = f\lambda$
   b. $d \sin\theta = n\lambda$
   c. $w = \lambda D / s$
   d. $\theta = \lambda / D$

3. An explorer pulls a sled at 30° to the horizontal with a force of 350 N but the friction of the snow resists the motion with a force of 90 N. The sled initially accelerates at 1.6 m s^{-2}.

   Calculate the sled's **mass**.

18th August

1 2 3

1. Sketch **sinusoidal** curves with double the frequency and twice the amplitude.

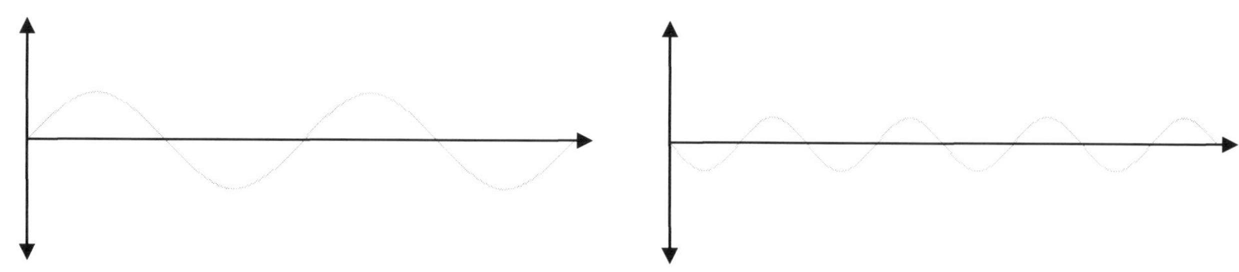

2. Rearrange the following to make **r** the subject:

   a. $V = kQ / r$

   b. $E = kQ / r^2$

   c. $F = kQ_1Q_2 / r^2$

   d. $F = GMm / r^2$

3. A large catapult has a spring constant of 6 000 N m^{-1} and is extended by 2.00 m. An object is fired vertically upwards and reaches a maximum height of 430 m.

   Calculate the **mass** of the object.

19th August

1 2 3

1. Sketch a **sinusoidal** curve on the axis below.

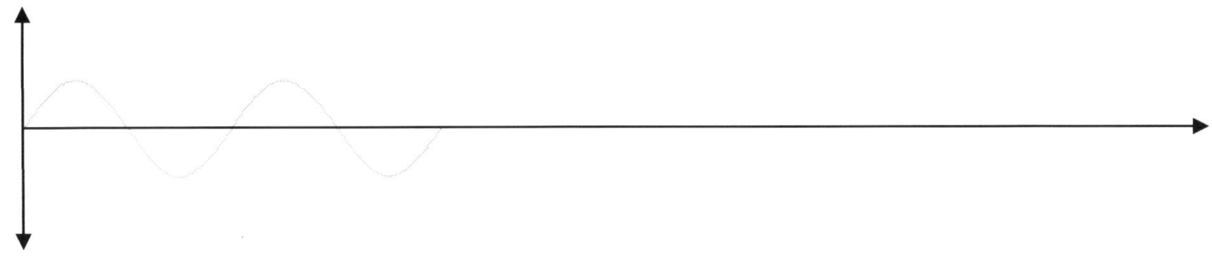

2. Write down the value of **A** if B = 54°.

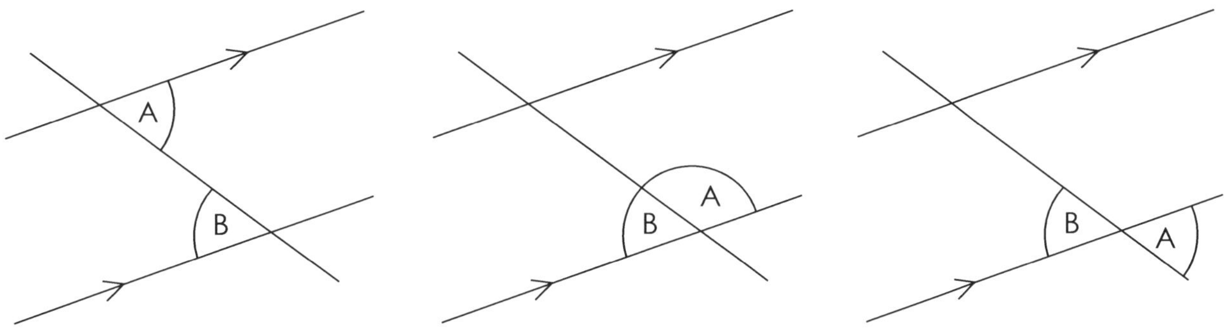

3. Below is part of a table of a student's results from a practical, which was repeated 5 times.

Force / N	2.2	2.3	2.2	1.2	2.1
Extension / mm	10	10	10	10	10

a. Identify the **anomaly**

b. Calculate the **average** force needed to extend the spring by 10 mm

20th August

1. Use one of the following symbols; <, <<, > or >>, to describe the **relationship** between the:
    a. Mass of the Earth and the mass of the Sun
    b. Mass of a proton and neutron
    c. Mass of a proton and an electron
    d. Mass of a black hole and the mass of the Sun

2. Calculate the value of **B** if A = 40˚.

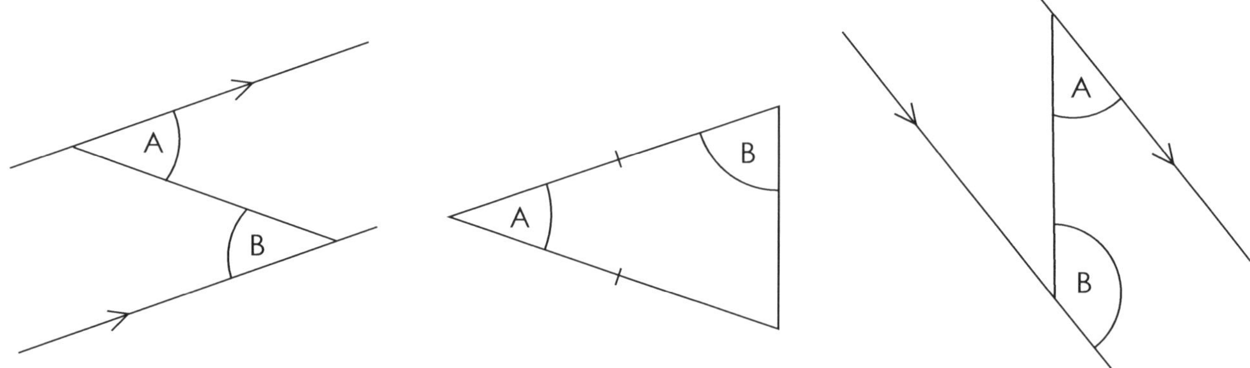

3. Using a wavefront diagram, explain how **refraction** occurs as a wave crosses a boundary between two media.

21st August

1 2 3

1. Sketch a **sinusoidal** curve on the axis below.

2. a. Write down the **sum** of A and B

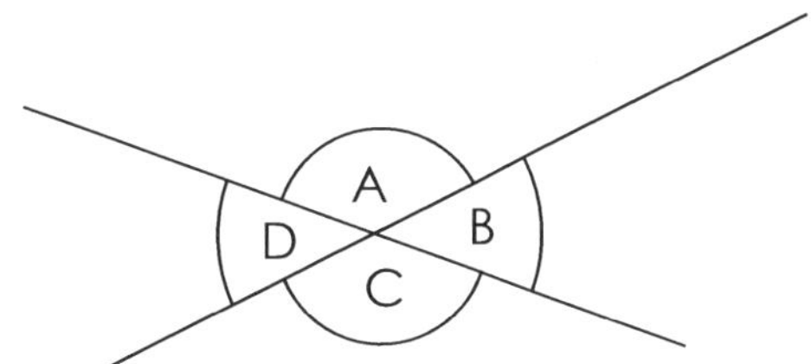

   b. Write down the value of **C** if D = 47°

3. A netball held at rest at a height of 1.45 m is dropped by a player. Calculate the **speed** of the ball just before it hits the floor and how **long** it takes to fall.

22nd August

1 2 3

1. Sketch a **sinusoidal** curve below – this should be better than the one you drew yesterday!

2. a. Write down the **relationship** between D and B

   b. Write down the value of **A** if C = 107°

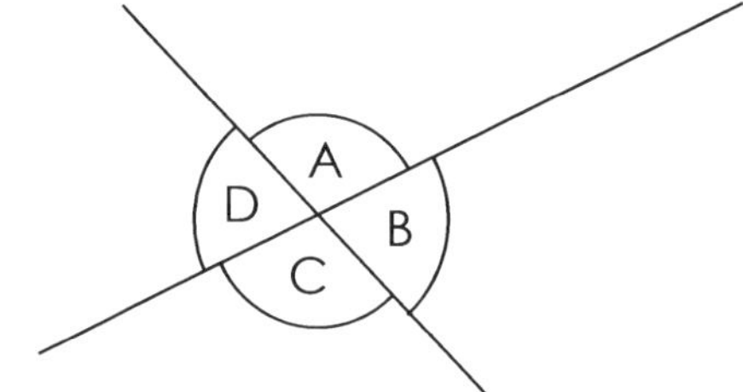

3. Write down the general formula for **alpha** decay on an element, X, with mass number, A, and atomic number, Z.

   Describe what happens in the nucleus when this occurs.

23rd August

1 2 3

1. Define the **conservation of linear momentum**.

2. Describe the phenomena of **reflection**. Include explanations for both specular and diffuse reflection.

3. Calculate the **depth** someone would need to dive to, in order to experience a pressure increase equal to that of atmospheric pressure.

(p_{atm} = 101 kPa and ρ_{water} = 1 000 kg m^{-3})

24th August

1 2 3

1. Define the **amplitude** of a wave.

2. Describe the **difference** between conventional DC current and how electrons move in a real circuit.

3. Explain why **increasing** the time over which a force acts, **decreases** the risk of injury during a crash. Include appropriate equations to help support your answer.

25th August

1 2 3

1. Define **longitudinal** and **transverse** waves – a diagram may be useful.

2. Describe the effect that decreasing the **volume** of a gas has on its **pressure** if the temperature remains constant. Explain why this happens.

3. Write down the general formula for **beta minus** decay of an element, X, with mass number, A, and atomic number, Z.

   Describe what happens in the nucleus when this occurs.

26th August

1 2 3

1. **Sketch** the graphs of $y = e^x$ and $y = e^{-x}$ on the same axis.

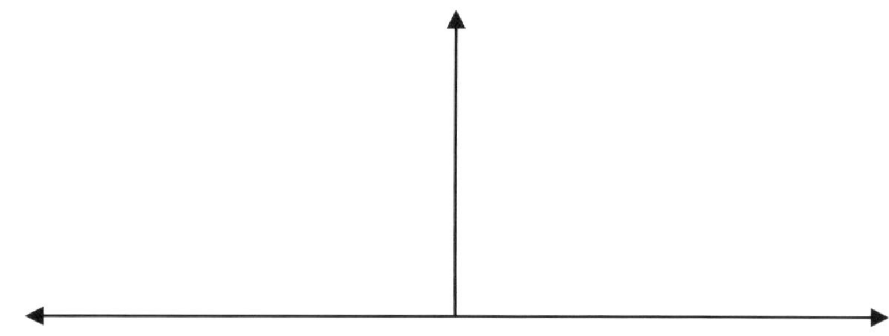

2. Describe the effect that decreasing the **temperature** of a gas has on its **pressure** if the volume remains constant. Explain why this happens.

3. A rocket, which has a mass of 3.00×10^5 kg accelerates vertically upwards such that it reaches a velocity of 200 m s^{-1} at a height of 5.00 km.

   Calculate the total **kinetic** and **gravitational potential** energy the rocket has gained from the chemical store of the rocket fuel, assuming its mass is unchanged and that the gravitational field strength is still 9.81 N kg^{-1} at that height.

27th August

1 2 3

1. Define **specific heat capacity**.

2. Describe the effect that increasing the **temperature** of a gas has on its **volume**, if the pressure remains constant. Explain why this happens.

3. Below is a table of results from a practical investigation with a spring.

   Plot the points on a graph and draw an **appropriate** line of best fit.

Extension / cm	Energy / J
1.0	4.0
2.0	15
3.0	36
4.0	48
5.0	98

28th August

1 2 3

1. Calculate **sinθ** for the following values of θ. Give your answers to 3 decimal places.
   a. 0˚
   b. 30˚
   c. 45˚
   d. 60˚
   e. 90˚

2. **Derive** the relationship between force and momentum from the equations for force ($F = ma$), acceleration ($a = \Delta v / t$) and momentum ($p = mv$).

3. A light ray passes into a transparent block of material from the air. The refractive index of the block is 1.4 and the angle of incidence is 45˚.

   Using Snell's Law ($n_1 \sin\theta_1 = n_2 \sin\theta_2$) calculate the **angle of refraction**.

29th August

1 2 3

1. Calculate **cosθ** for the following values of θ. Give your answers to 3 decimal places.
   a. 0°
   b. 30°
   c. 45°
   d. 60°
   e. 90°

2. Describe how an object can **accelerate** if its **speed** is **constant**.

3. Two resistors, of resistance 40 Ω and 60 Ω, are connected in parallel to a 1.5 V cell.

   Calculate the **current** through each resistor and the total current drawn from the cell.

30th August - Part 1

1. Trace the following **curves**.

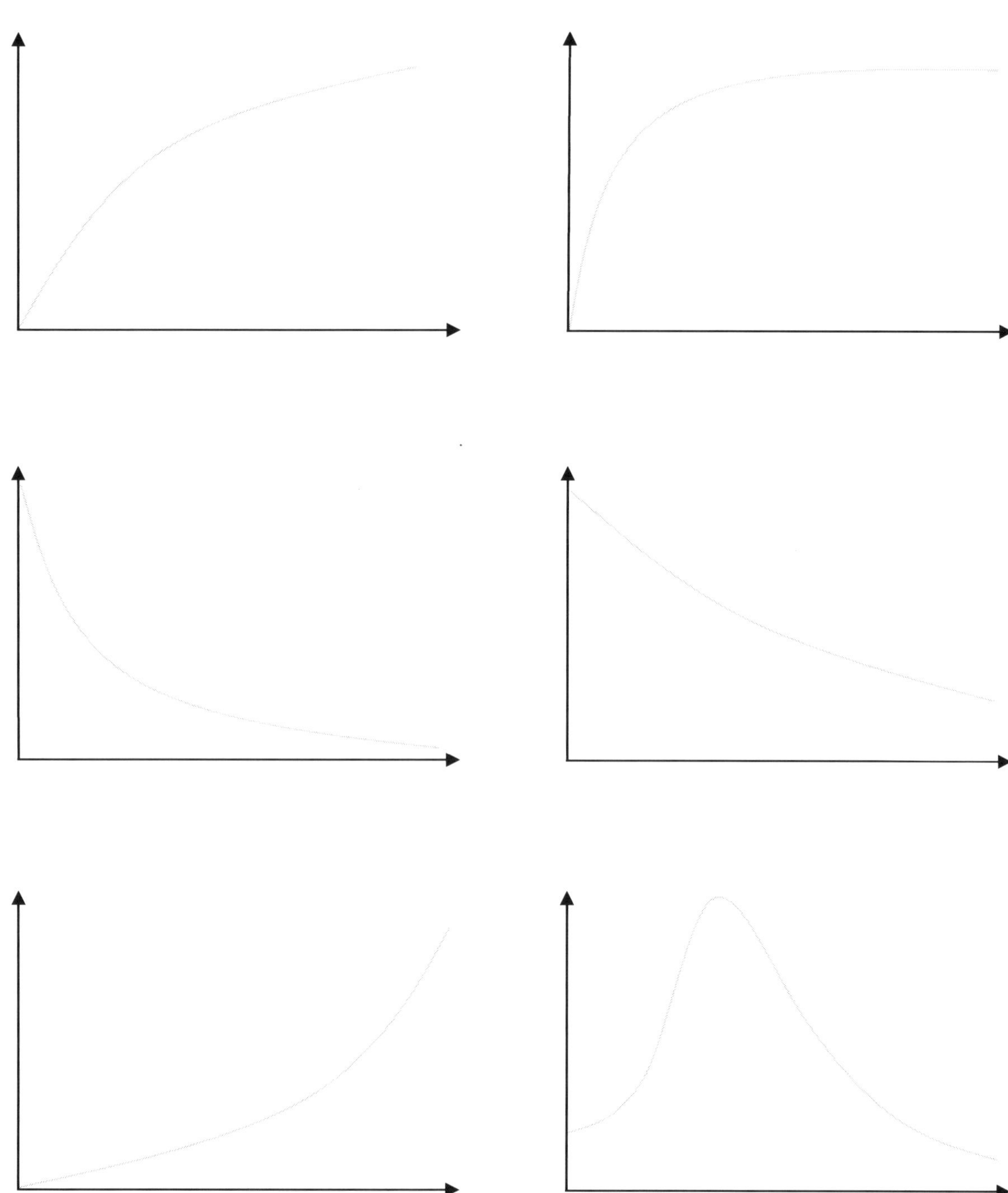

30th August - Part 2

2. Draw an appropriate **line of best fit** for the following graphs.

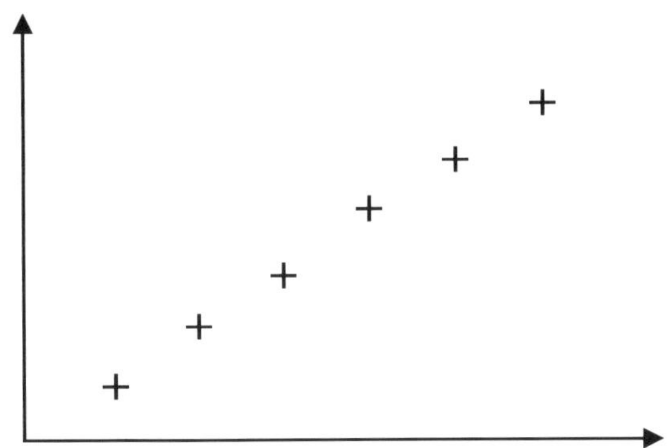

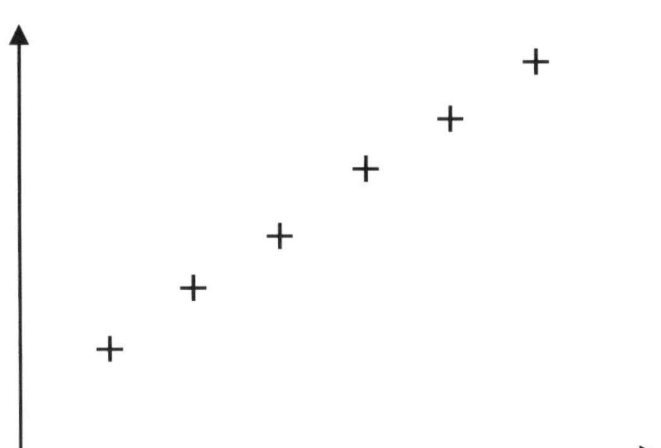

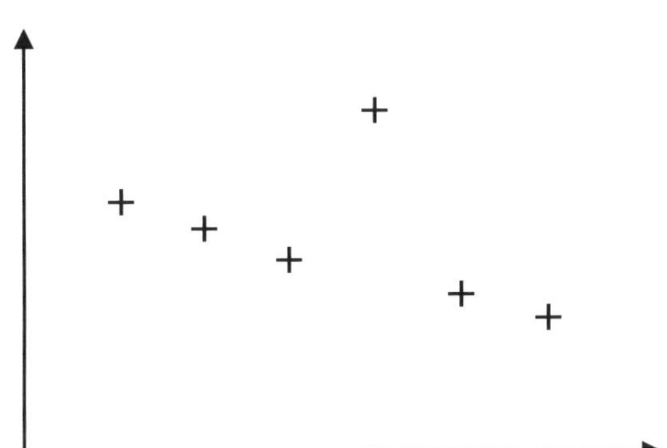

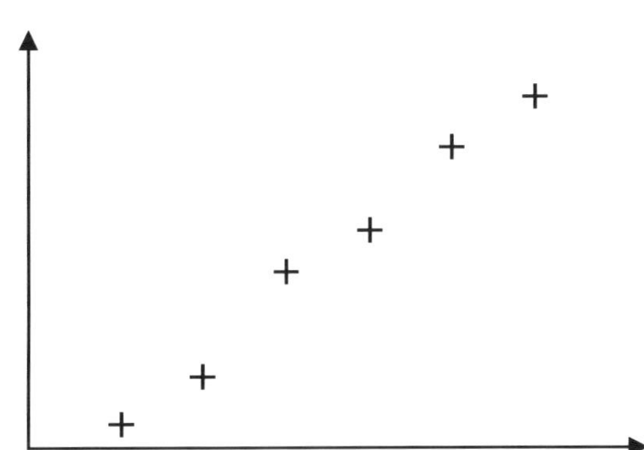

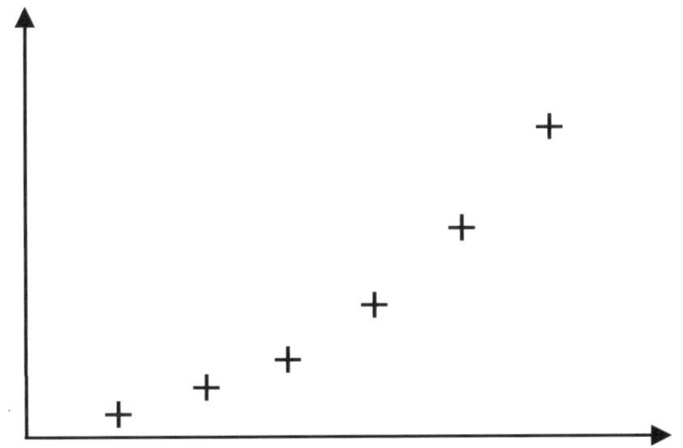

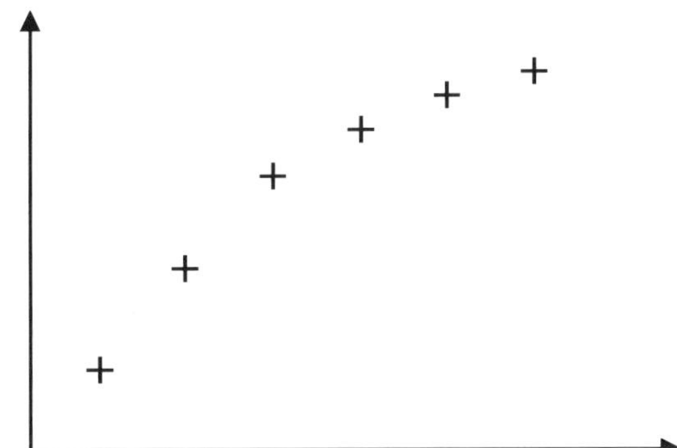

31st August - Part 1

1. Trace the following **curves**.

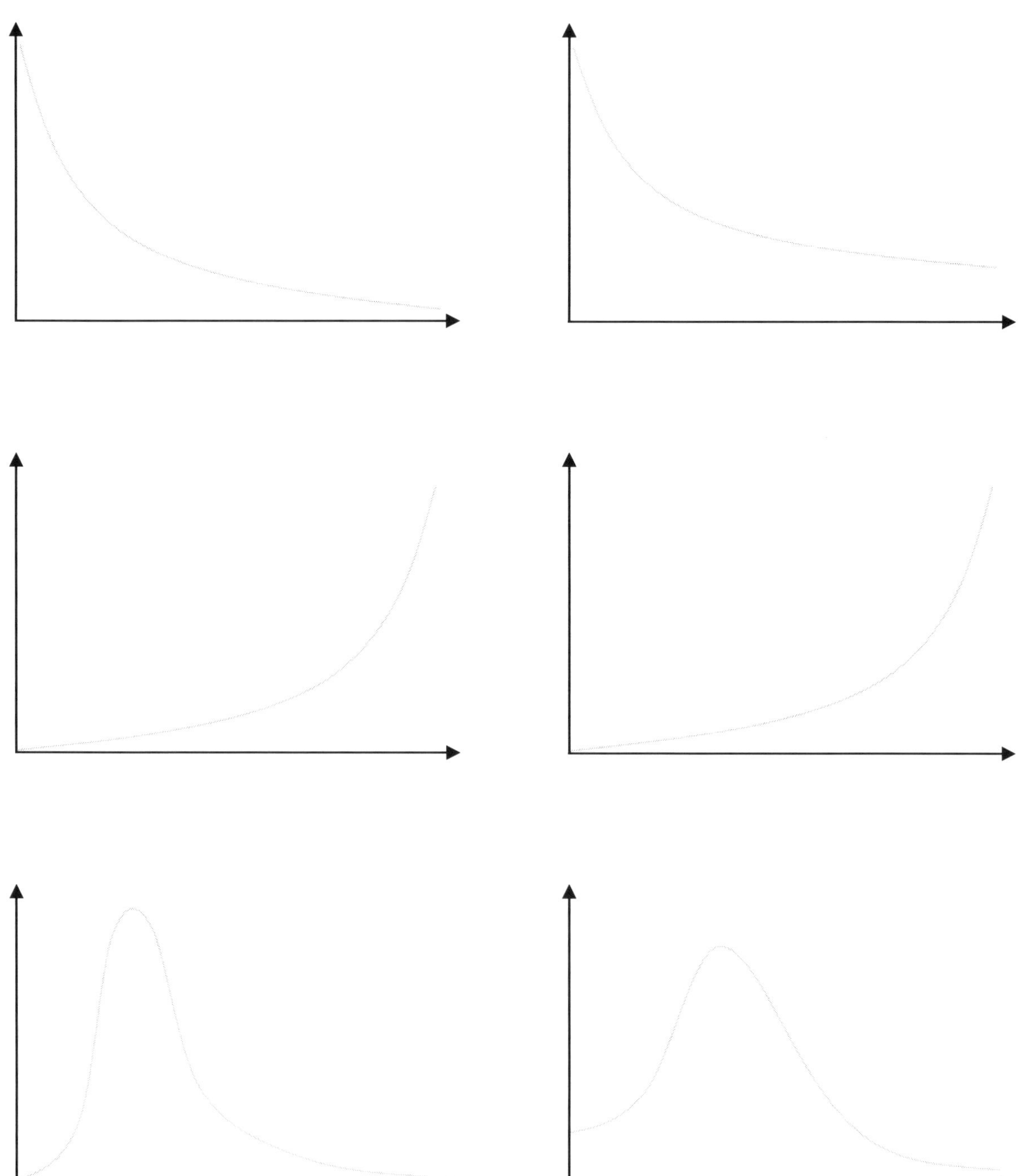

31st August - Part 2

2

2. Draw an appropriate **line of best fit** for the following graphs.

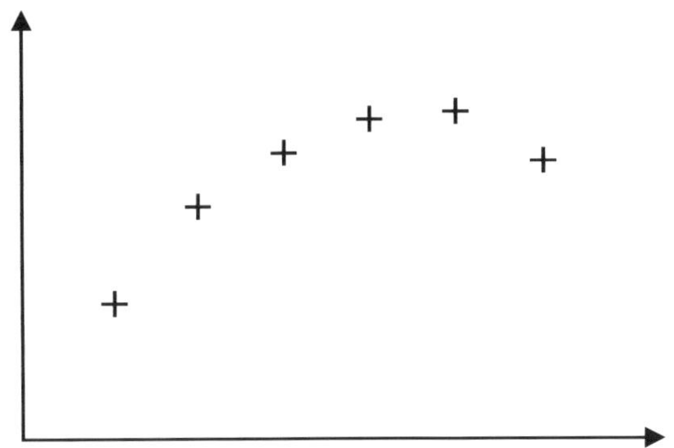
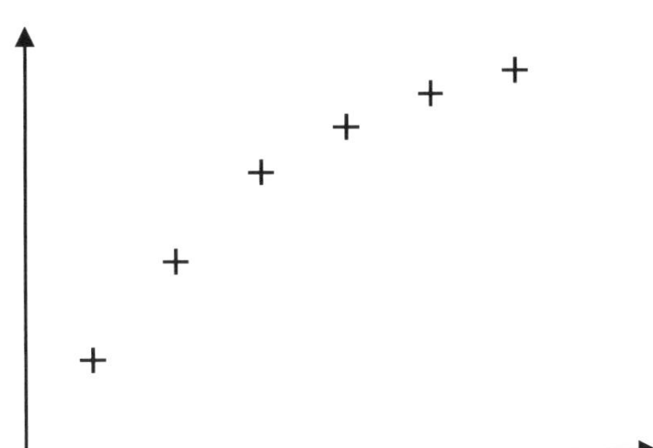
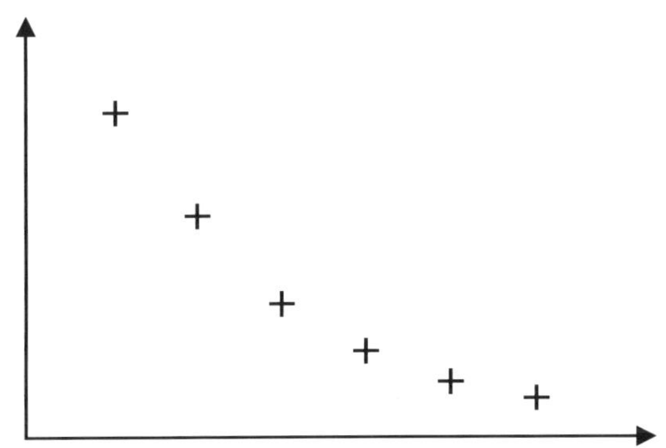
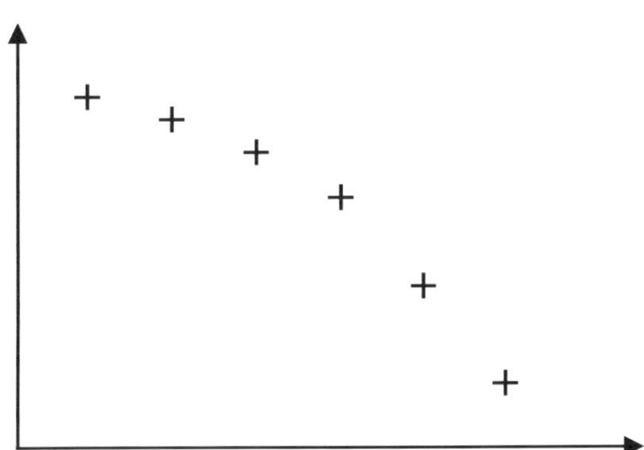
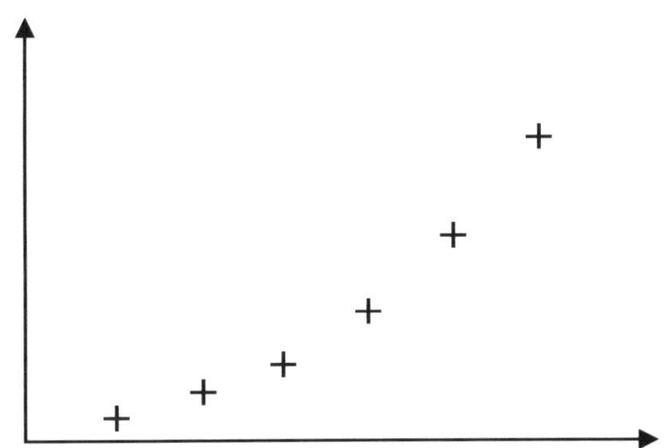
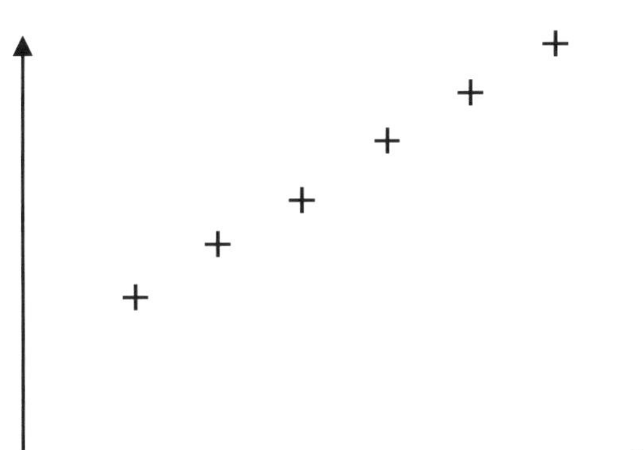

AUGUST REVIEW

Just like in July, reflect on the progress you have made and have another go at any questions you may have missed this month.

A Level Physics Content	Red	Amber	Green
I can convert from prefixes to **SI units**.			
I can complete vector diagrams to work out the **magnitude** and **direction** of the resultant vector by **scale drawing**.			
I can calculate the cross-sectional area of a **circle**.			
I can calculate the surface area and volume of a **sphere**.			
I can sketch a **sinusoidal** curve.			
I can draw an appropriate **line of best fit**.			

Any other comments:

SEPTEMBER

SEPTEMBER

It's going to begin soon!

This can be a challenging time as you meet new teachers and the work is a step up from GCSE – stay positive, you will quickly learn to adapt.

Make sure you have the following equipment so you're prepared for your first few lessons:

- Pens
- Pencil, rubber and sharpener
- A4 ring binders
- Scientific calculator
- 30 cm clear ruler
- Compass
- Protractor
- Two set squares

1st September

1 2 3

1. Calculate the **angle**, θ, in the triangle with an opposite side length of 6.50 m and an adjacent side length of 8.00 m.

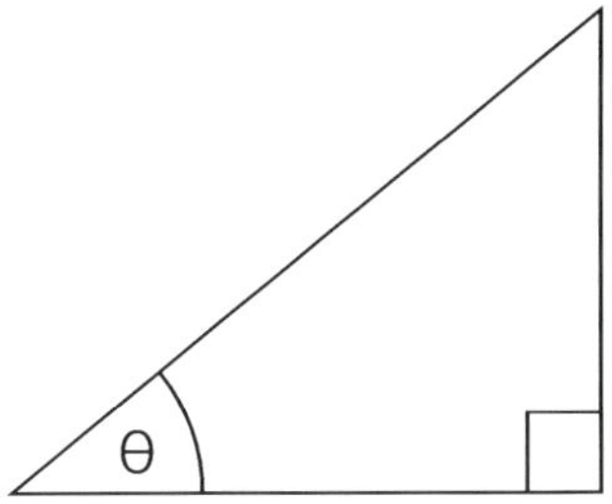

2. Write the following derived unit in terms of SI Base Units (kg, m, s etc): **newton**

3. Describe the **similarities** and **differences** between transverse and longitudinal waves giving examples of each.

2nd September

1 2 3

1. Calculate the length of the **hypotenuse** of a triangle with an angle θ of 72° and an opposite side length of 5.4 cm.

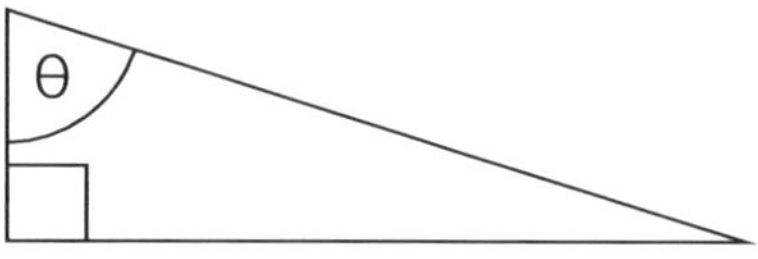

2. Write the following derived unit in terms of SI Base Units: **joule**

3. Describe the **similarities** and **differences** between mechanical and electromagnetic waves giving examples of each.

3rd September

1 2 3

1. Calculate the length of the **adjacent** side of a triangle with an angle θ of 80° and a hypotenuse length of 0.40 m.

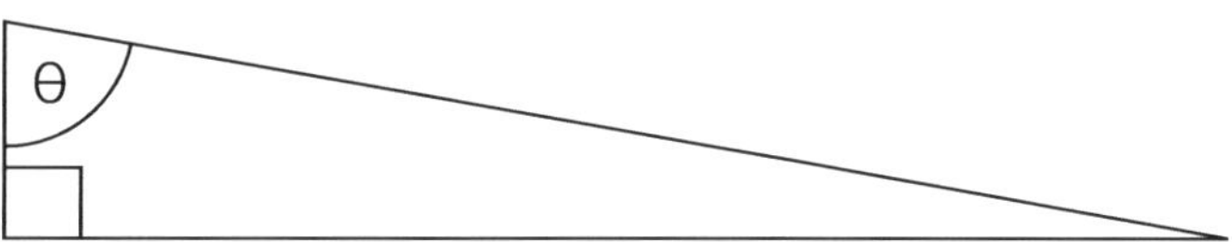

2. Write the following derived unit in terms of SI Base Units: **volt**

3. State **Hooke's Law** and describe how it could be investigated in the lab.

4th September

1 2 3

1. Calculate the length of the **opposite** side of a right-angled triangle if the hypotenuse is 380 mm and the adjacent side is 70 mm. Draw a diagram to help.

2. Write the following derived unit in terms of SI Base Units: **pascal**

3. Determine **θ** if A = 58°.

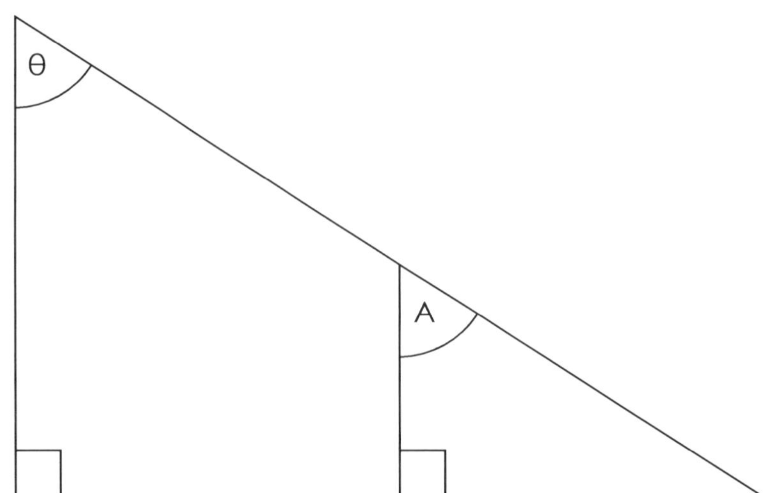

5th September

1 2 3

1. Calculate the **diagonal** length of a square with a side length of 7.00 cm.

2. Write the following derived unit in terms of SI Base Units: **tesla**

3. Calculate **θ** if A = 23˚.

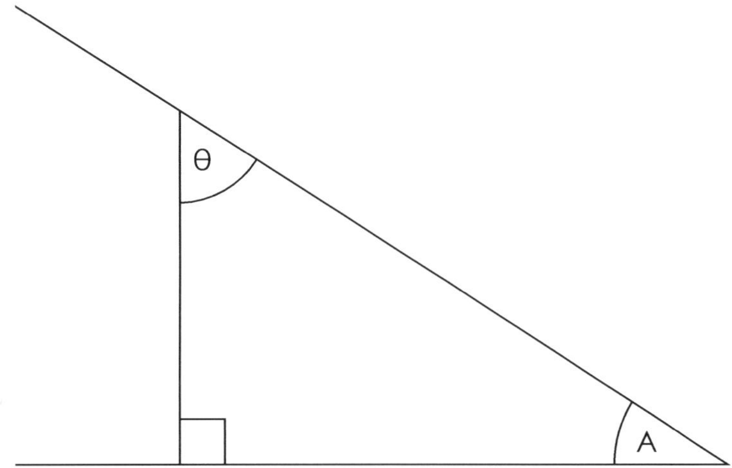

6th September

1 2 3

1. Calculate, **without** using a calculator:
    a. 3.0×10^4 multiplied by 3.0×10^7
    b. 4.0×10^5 multiplied by 2.0×10^7
    c. 3.0×10^{-2} multiplied by 3.0×10^{-7}
    d. 3.0×10^4 multiplied by 4.0×10^{-6}

2. Define what is meant by a **vector** and list six vector quantities.

3. Calculate θ if A = 24°.

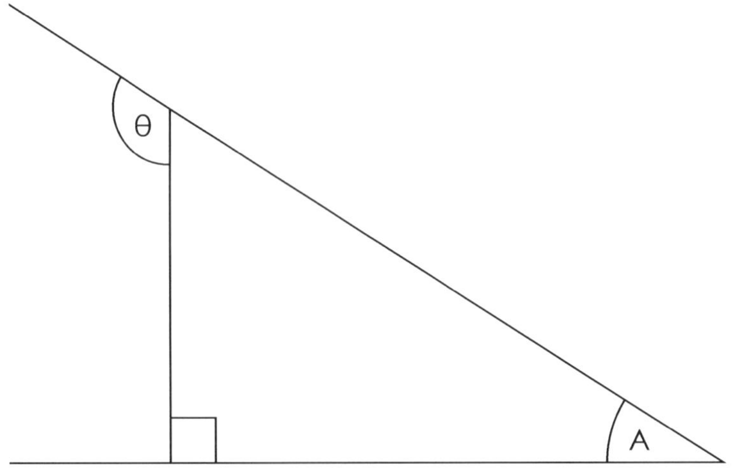

7th September

1 2 3

1. Sketch a **sinusoidal** curve on the axis below.

2. Define the **work done** on an object.

3. Calculate **θ** if A = 19.2˚.

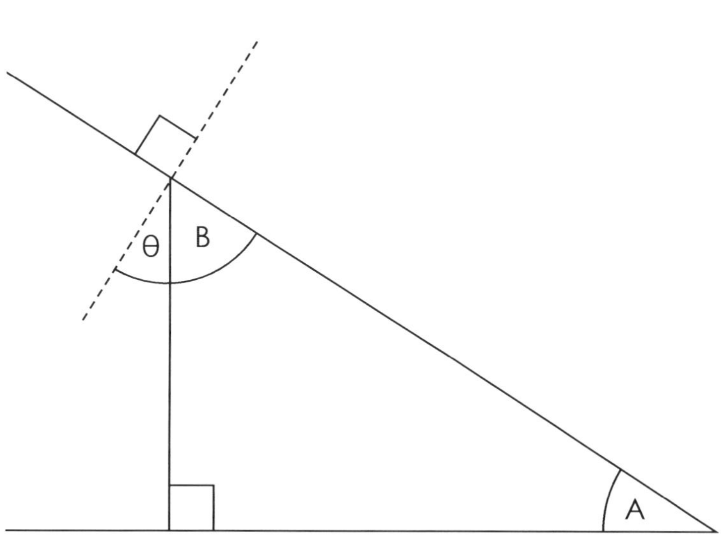

8th September

1 2 3

1. Calculate the **wavelength** of a wave that is travelling at 520 m s^{-1} and has a time period of 13.0 s.

2. **Sketch** the graph of y = -2x + 11.

3. Draw a sinusoidal wave on a **displacement-distance** graph with a wavelength of 5.0 cm and amplitude 20 mm. Label the wavelength and amplitude on your diagram.

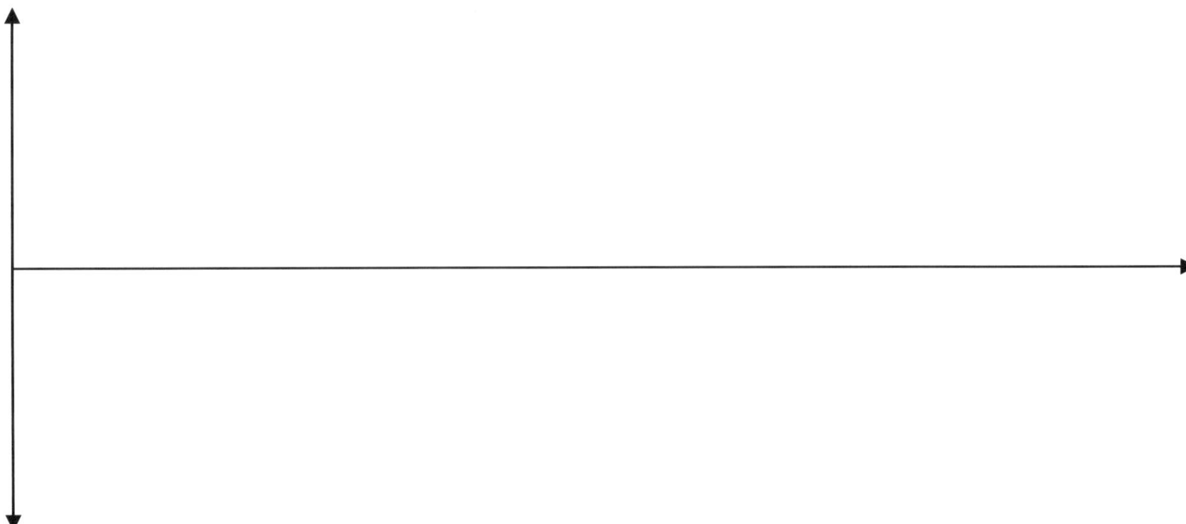

9th September

1 2 3

1. State **Newton's three laws of motion** (from memory if you can).

   - 1st Law

   - 2nd Law

   - 3rd Law

2. Form expressions for sides **P** and **L** in terms of θ and W.

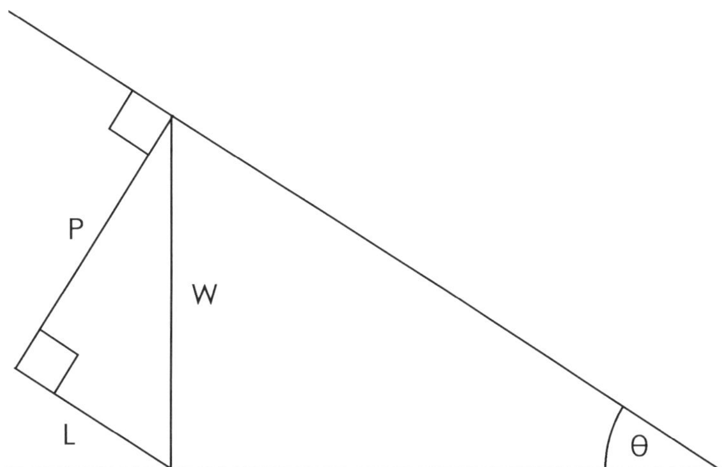

10th September

1 2 3

1. Solve $\frac{1}{x} = \frac{1}{2} + \frac{1}{3}$ for **x**.

2. Find out what these numbers **represent**:
   a. 9.11×10^{-31} kg
   b. 8.85×10^{-12} F m^{-1}
   c. 1.661×10^{-27} kg
   d. 1.60×10^{-19} C
   e. 6.63×10^{-34} J s
   f. 1.60×10^{-19} J

3. Calculate the **magnitude** of P and L if θ = 29.3° and W = 105.

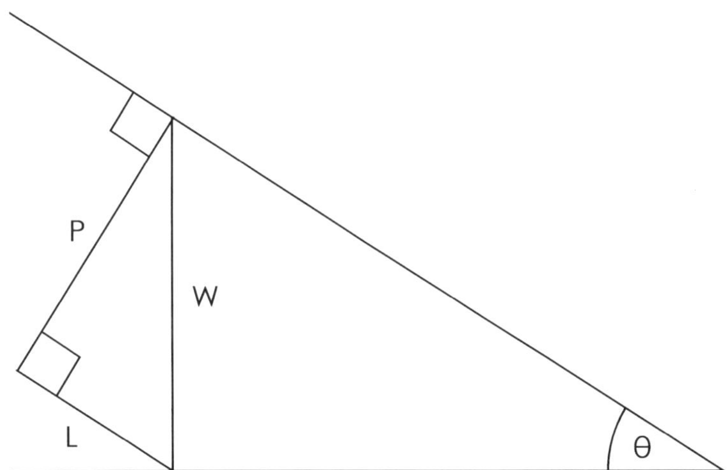

11th September

1 2 3

1. Solve $\frac{1}{x} = \frac{1}{20} + \frac{1}{60}$ for **x**.

2. Identify what the **area** underneath the following graphs represents:

   a. A force-extension graph

   b. A velocity-time graph

   c. A force-time graph

3. Form expressions for the **parallel** and **perpendicular** components (relative to the slope) of the block's weight, W, in terms of θ.

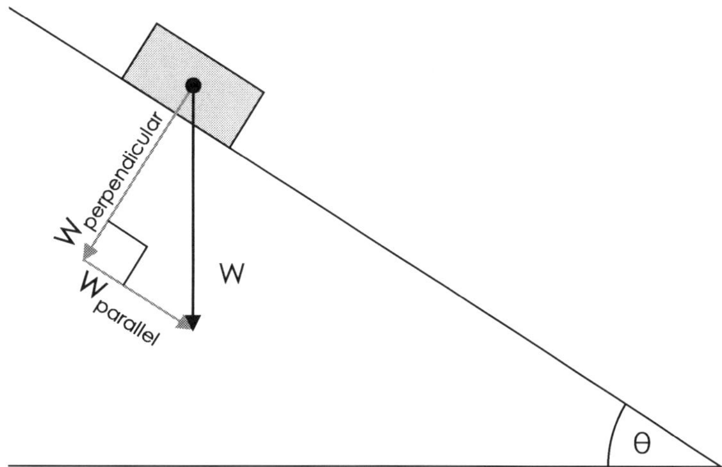

12th September

1. Solve $\frac{1}{x} = \frac{1}{45} + \frac{1}{25} + \frac{1}{15}$ for **x**.

2. Identify the following electrical **components**:

3. Calculate the **parallel** and **perpendicular** components of the weight of the block if it has a weight of 10.0 N and the slope is at an angle of 29.0° to the bench.

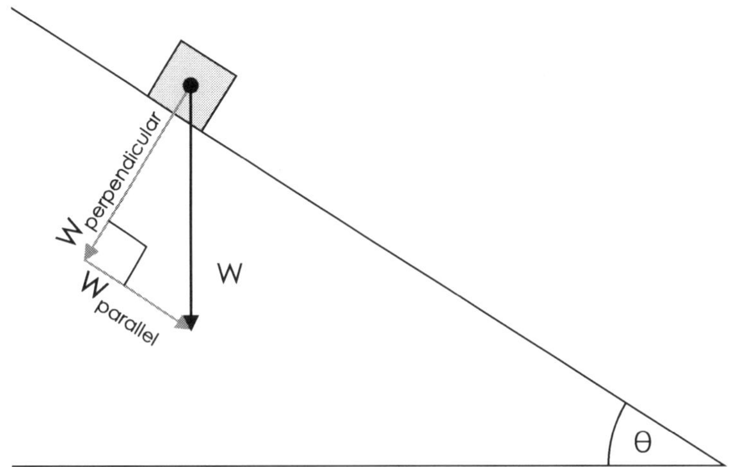

13th September

1 2 3

1. Combine into one fraction and rearrange $\frac{1}{x} = \frac{1}{A} + \frac{1}{B}$ to make **x** the subject.

2. Calculate the **area** under the graph of y = 3x + 3 between x = 0 and x = 3. Sketching the graph may help.

3. Calculate the **parallel** and **perpendicular** components of the block's weight if m = 71.0 kg and θ = 38˚.

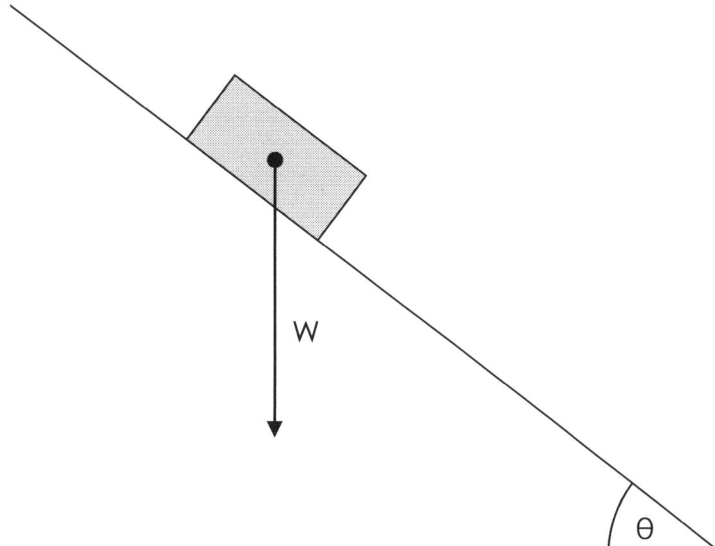

14th September

1 2 3

1. Write down a definition for an **ohmic conductor**.

2. Complete the **tip-to-tail** vector diagrams by drawing in the resultant vector and working out the magnitude and direction of the resultant force.

a.

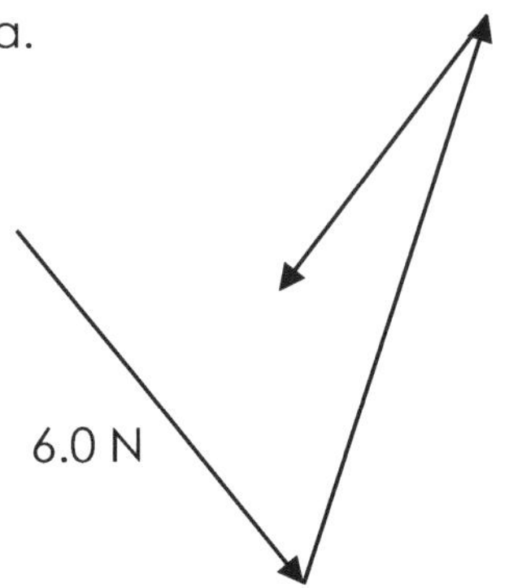

b.

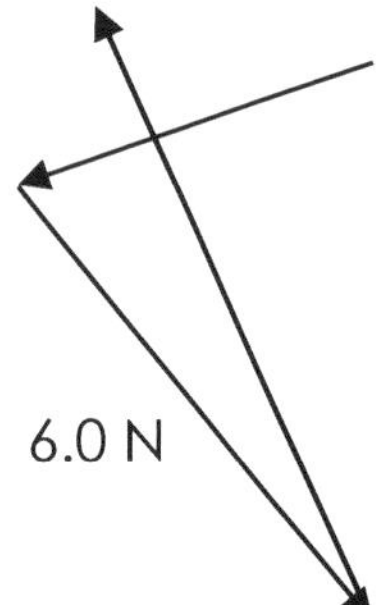

c.

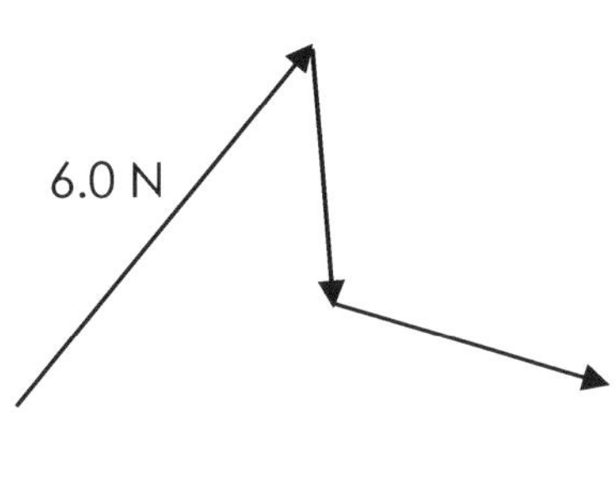

3. Draw a sinusoidal wave on a **displacement-time** graph with a frequency of 50 Hz and amplitude 40 mm. Label the time period and amplitude on your diagram.

15th September

1. Complete the **circuit symbol** for:

   a. A thermistor

   b. An LDR

   c. A variable resistor

   d. A fuse

   e. A heater

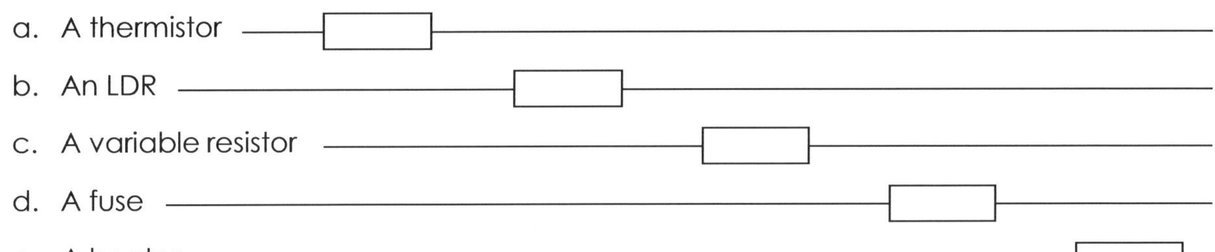

2. Complete the vector diagram by using the **parallelogram** method to draw in the resultant vector. Write in its magnitude (to 1 d.p.) and angle from the vertical.

   a.

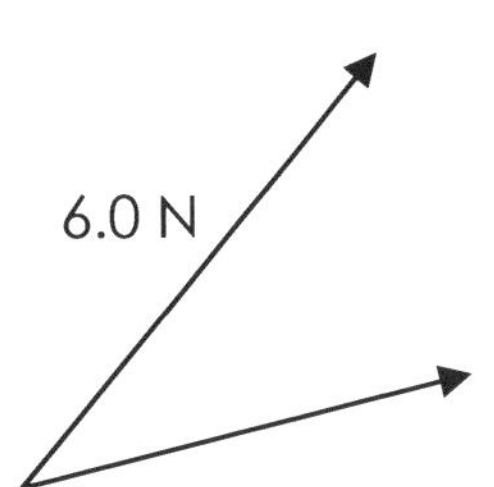

   b.

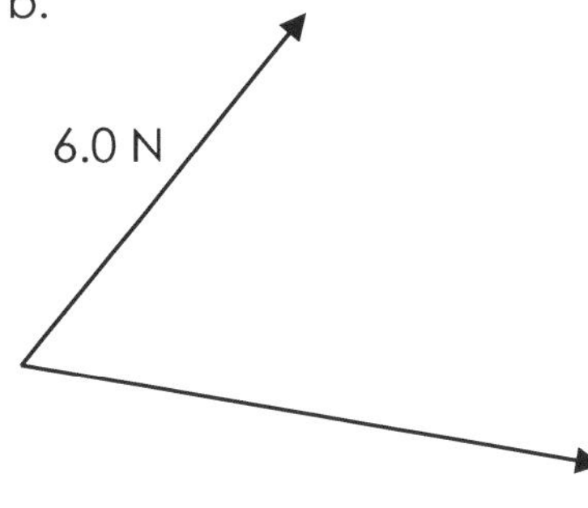

3. Describe the difference between **scalars** and **vectors** and give six examples of each.

16th September

1. Complete the **circuit symbol** for:
   a. An ammeter
   b. A voltmeter

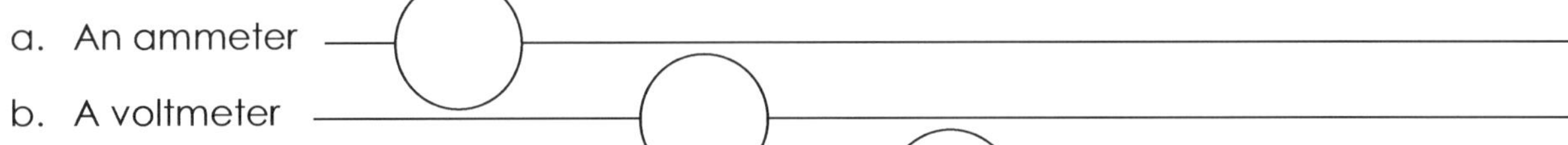

   c. A galvanometer

   d. A motor
   e. An LED

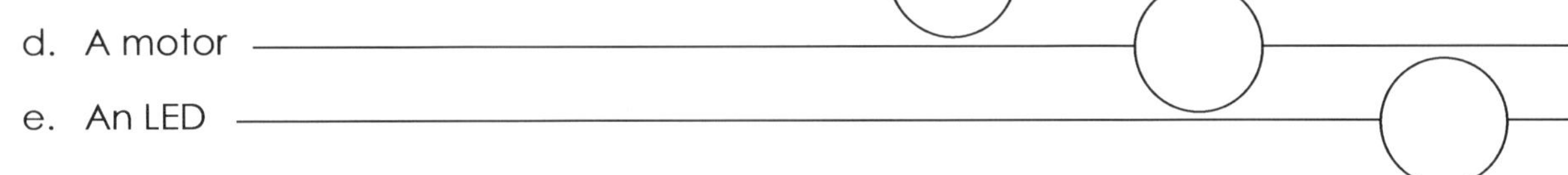

2. Discuss the **energy changes** in a ball that is dropped and then bounces.

3. Calculate, using a **graphical** method, the size and angle to the vertical of the resultant force produced by these two perpendicular forces:

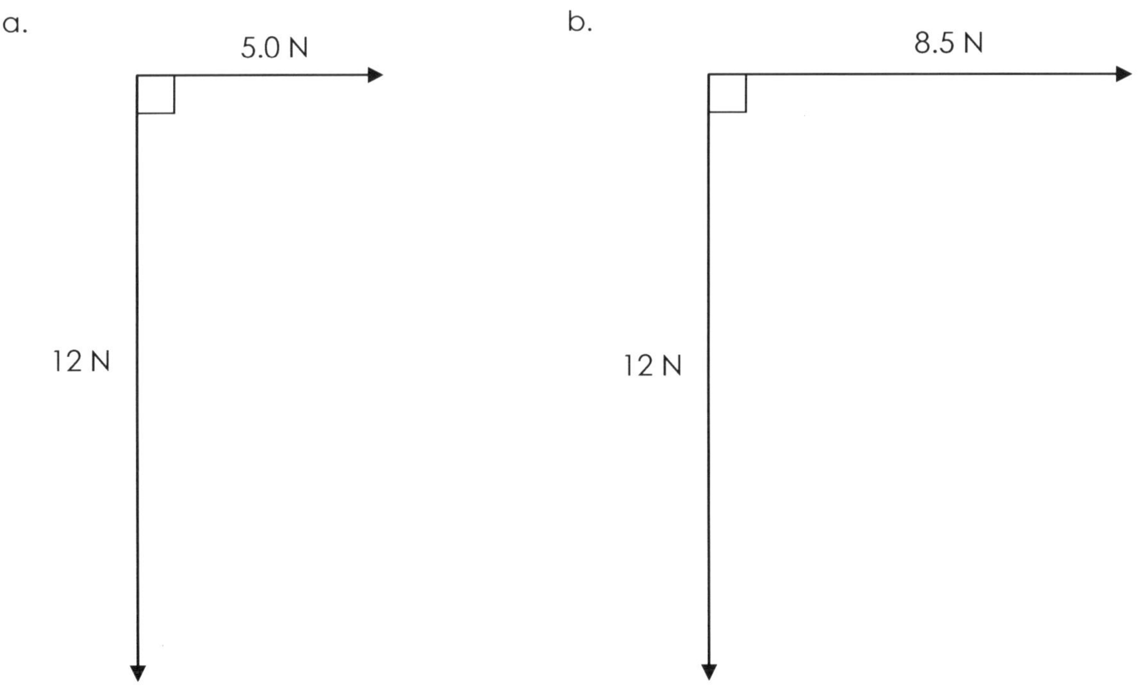

17th September

1. Use one of the following symbols, <, <<, > or >>, to describe the relationship between the **momentum** of a flying flying squirrel and the **momentum** of a flying bee.

2. Calculate the **speed** a 162 g hockey ball will be travelling when it hits the ground from the top of the Shard if you ignore air resistance. The Shard is 310m tall.

   Explain why, in reality, the ball will never reach this speed.

3. Calculate, using a **mathematical** method, the size and angle to the vertical of the resultant force produced by these two perpendicular forces.

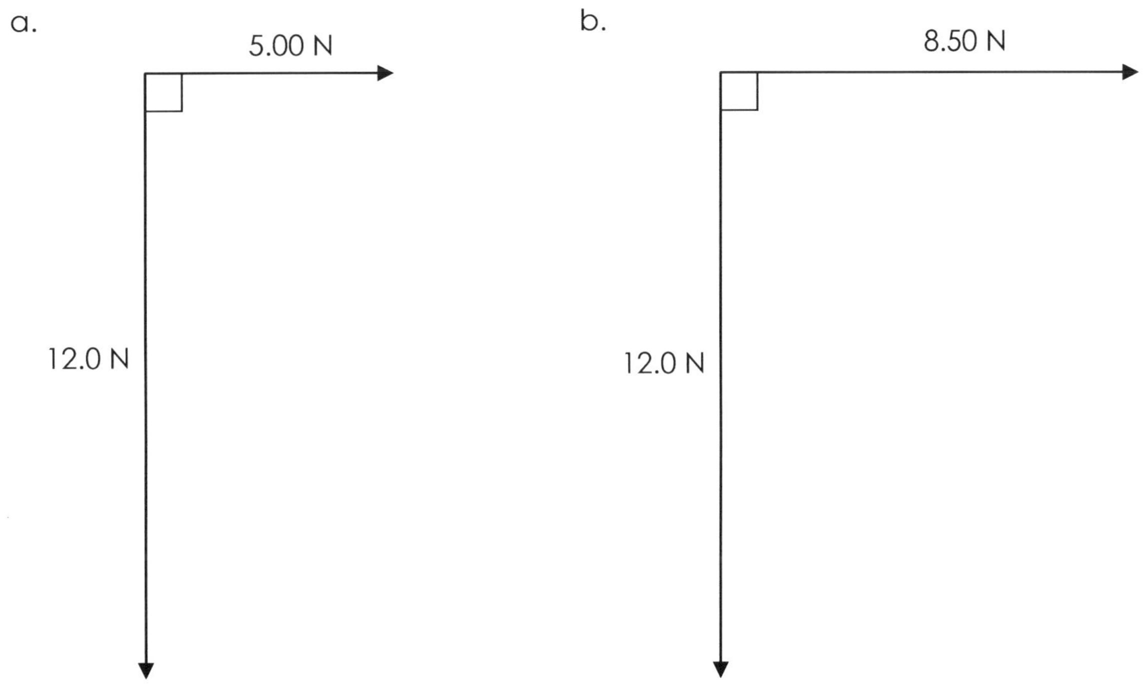

18th September

1 2 3

1. Write down the **units** for:
   a. Momentum
   b. Pressure
   c. Activity
   d. Magnetic flux density

2. An object of mass 2.0 kg is launched vertically upwards by a catapult to a height of 57 m. The catapult has a spring constant of 1 800 N m^{-1}.

   Calculate the **extension** of the catapult to achieve this.

3. Calculate the size of the resultant force to the nearest 100 N, using **scale drawing**, produced by a vertical force of 8.90 kN and a horizontal force of 16.3 kN.

19th September

1 2 3

1. List ten **types** of force.

2. Explain why it is better to use a **monochromatic** light source when studying refraction.

3. Calculate the size and direction of the resultant force, using a **mathematical** method, produced by an upwards vertical force of 92 578 N and a horizontal force of 125 287 N to the left.

20th September

1 2 3

1. Rearrange the following to make $\mathbf{V_p}$ the subject:

   a. $V_p / V_s = n_p / n_s$

   b. $V_pI_p = V_sI_s$

2. The number of turns of a transformer is 300 on the primary coil and 100 on the secondary coil. The potential difference across the primary coil is 6.0 V.

   Calculate the **potential difference** across the secondary coil and state the type of transformer used.

3. A 2.50 tonne Landrover is initially moving at 18 m s^{-1}. It takes 24.0 m to come to a complete stop.

   Calculate the average **braking force** required and describe what happens to the kinetic energy of the car as it slows down.

21st September

1 2 3

1. Calculate the **area**, in m^2, of a circle with:
   a. Radius 2.42 mm
   b. Diameter 1.12 mm
   c. Diameter 181 μm
   d. Diameter 3.14 m

2. Calculate the **current** if:
   a. 300 mC of charge moves past a point every 0.50 s
   b. A 20 W heater has a potential difference of 24 V across it
   c. A 20 W heater has a resistance of 47 Ω

3. Explain the **difference** between:
   a. Distance and displacement
   b. Speed and velocity
   c. Gravity and weight

22nd September

1 2 3

1. Combine into one fraction and rearrange $1/R_T = 1/R_1 + 1/R_2$ to make $\mathbf{R_T}$ the subject.

2. Calculate the **total resistance** of a 13 Ω and 18 Ω resistor if connected in:

   a. Series

   a. Parallel

3. Two cars have masses $m_1 = 1500$ kg and $m_2 = 2000$ kg. They travel in opposite directions at 1.0 m s^{-1} and 6.0 m s^{-1} respectively. They collide and move off together.

   Calculate the **final velocity** of the two cars after they crash.

23rd September

1 2 3

1. Calculate the **gradient** and **y-intercept** of the line with equation:
   a. $3y = 9x - 3$
   b. $3y + 9x = -3$
   c. $3y^2 - 3y = 9yx$
   d. $y = 3(x + 3)$

2. Calculate the **total resistance** of a 13 Ω, 20 Ω and 18 Ω resistor if connected in:
   a. Series

   a. Parallel

3. A 10 Ω resistor is connected to a 6.0 V battery.

   Describe the **effect** (including **values**) that adding another 20 Ω resistor in **series** has on:

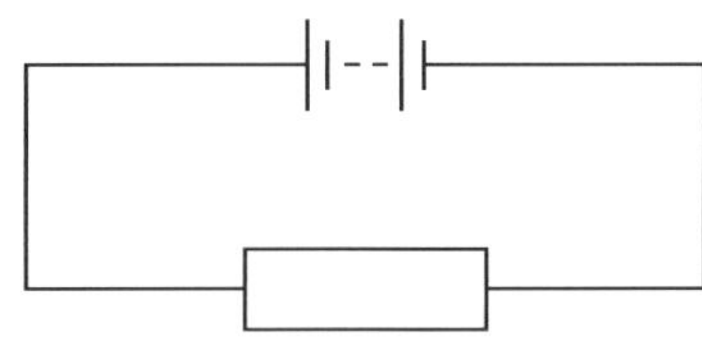

a. The total resistance

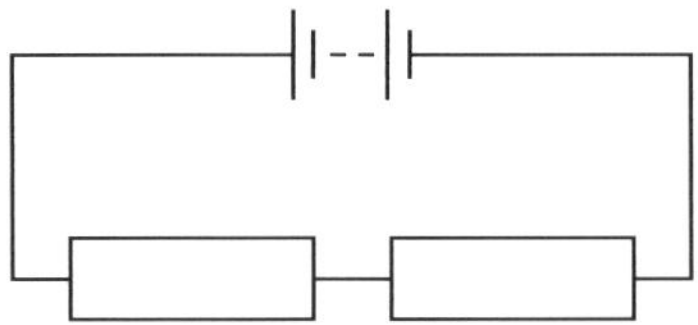

b. The current

c. The potential difference across each component

24th September

1 2 3

1. Write down the **units** for:
   a. Acceleration
   b. Density
   c. Spring constant
   d. Moment

2. By taking the minimum radio wave frequency as 1.0 Hz and the maximum gamma ray frequency as 1.0×10^{20} Hz, calculate the **ratio** between the range of visible light frequencies and the whole EM spectrum.

3. A 10 Ω resistor is connected to a 6.0 V battery.

   Describe the **effect** (including **values**) that adding another 20 Ω resistor in **parallel** has on:

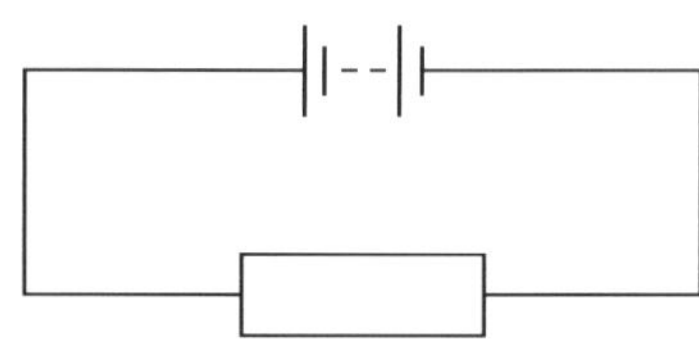

   a. The total resistance

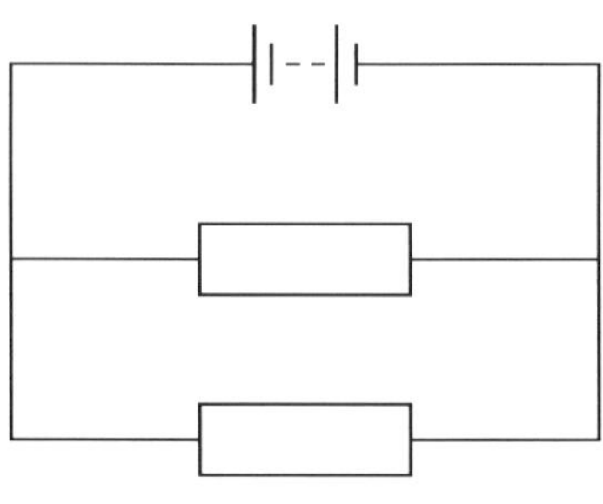

   b. The total current

   c. The potential difference across each component

25th September

1 2 3

1. Write down the **units** for:
    a. Acceleration due to gravity
    b. Specific heat capacity
    c. Specific latent heat
    d. Gravitational field strength

2. Describe how metals **conduct** electricity.

3. A ray of light is shone into a block of unknown material from air at an angle of 23° to the normal and refracts at an angle of 15°. Calculate the **refractive index** of the material and hence the **speed of light** in the material.

26th September

1 2 3

1. Sketch a **sinusoidal** curve on the axis below.

2. Sketch the **IV graph** for a filament lamp, ohmic resistor and diode.

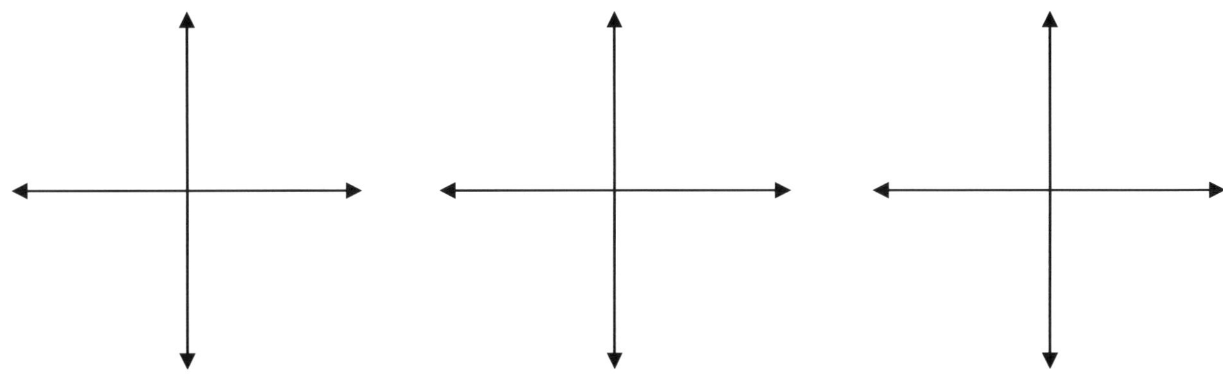

3. Calculate the **gradient** of the following line.

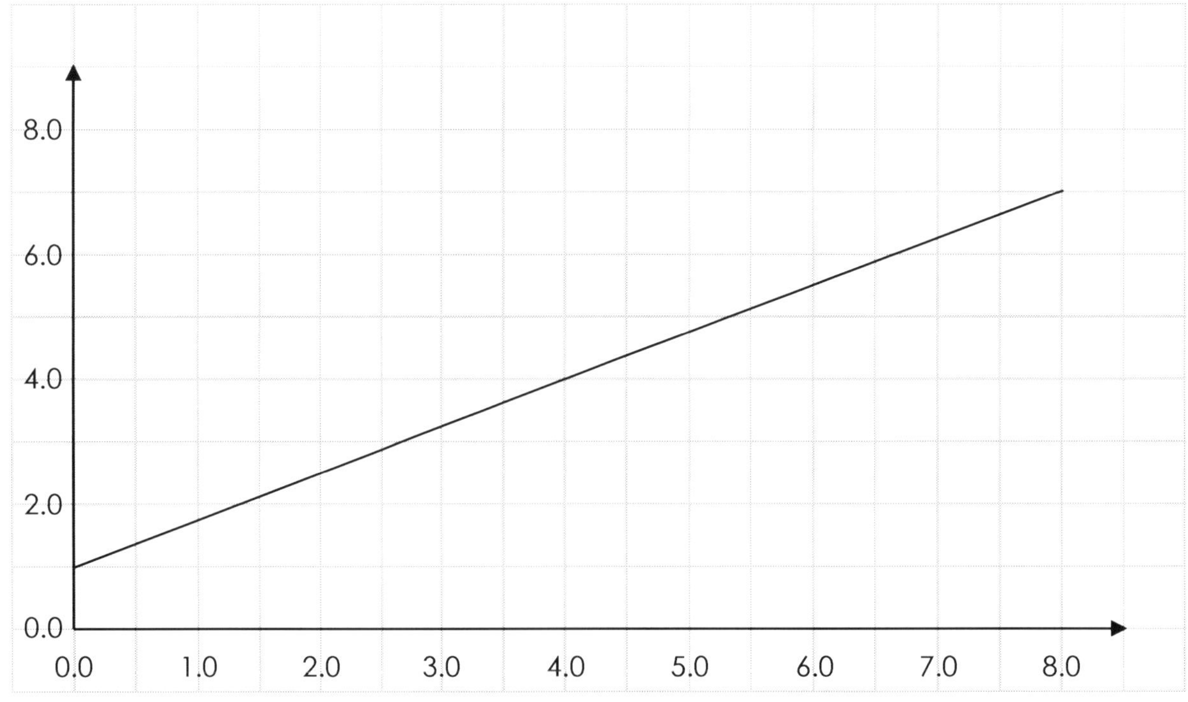

27th September

1 2 3

1. Calculate the gradient and hence the **equation** of the straight-line graph that goes through the points (5, 2) and (9, 1).

2. Sketch the **IV graph** for three different resistors of increasing resistance.

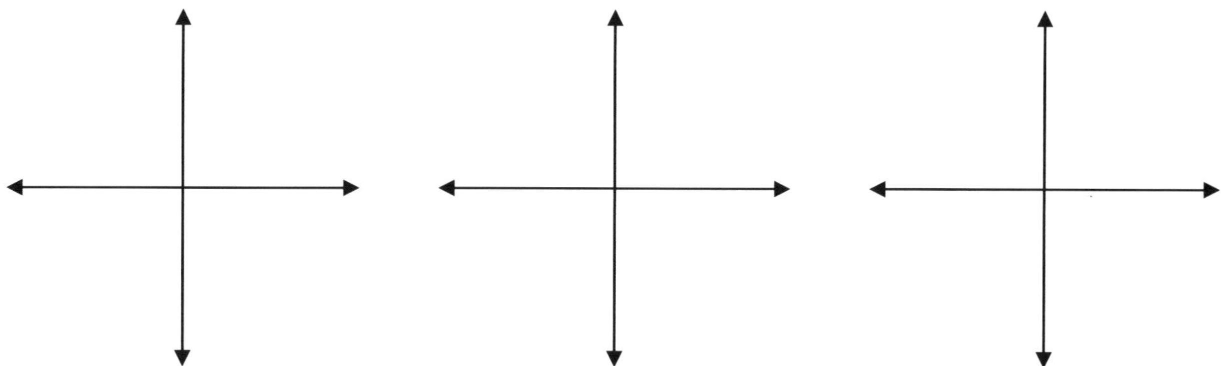

3. Calculate the **gradient** of the following data, giving an appropriate unit.

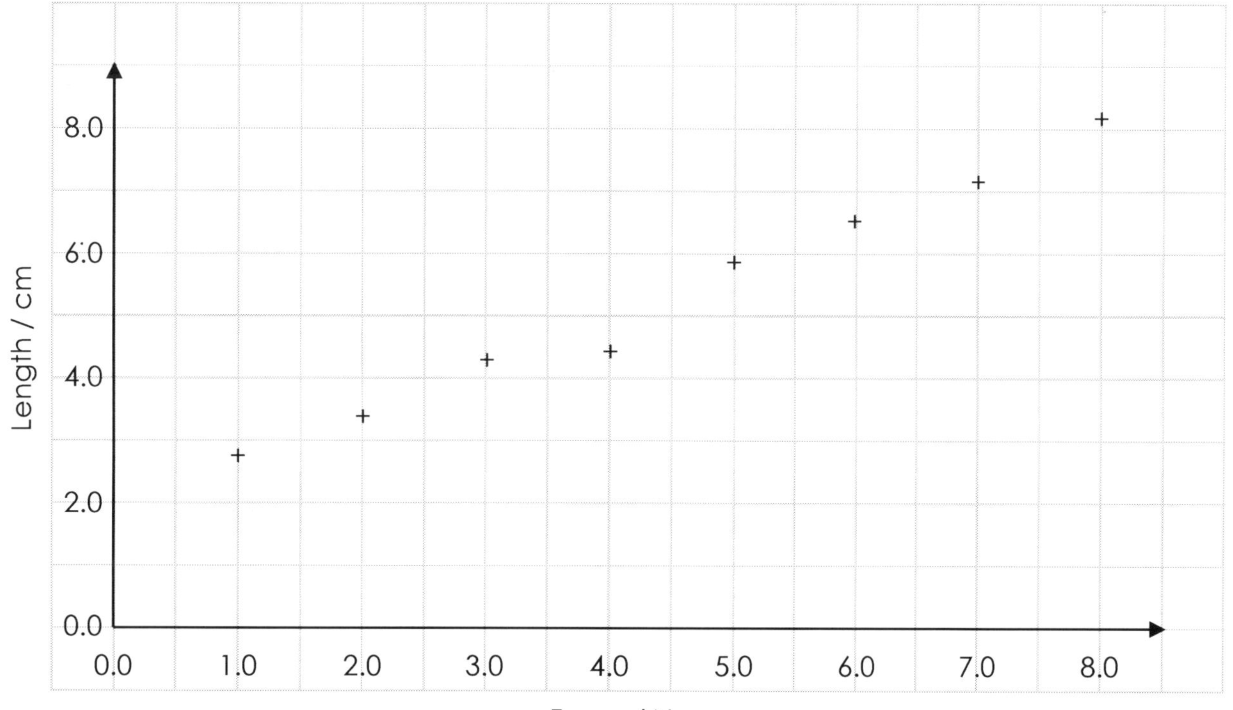

28th September

1 2 3

1. Calculate the **equation** of the straight-line graph that goes through the point (0, 4) and has a gradient of -0.1.

2. Sketch the **IV graph** of a metal wire at a constant temperature, a red LED and a blue LED.

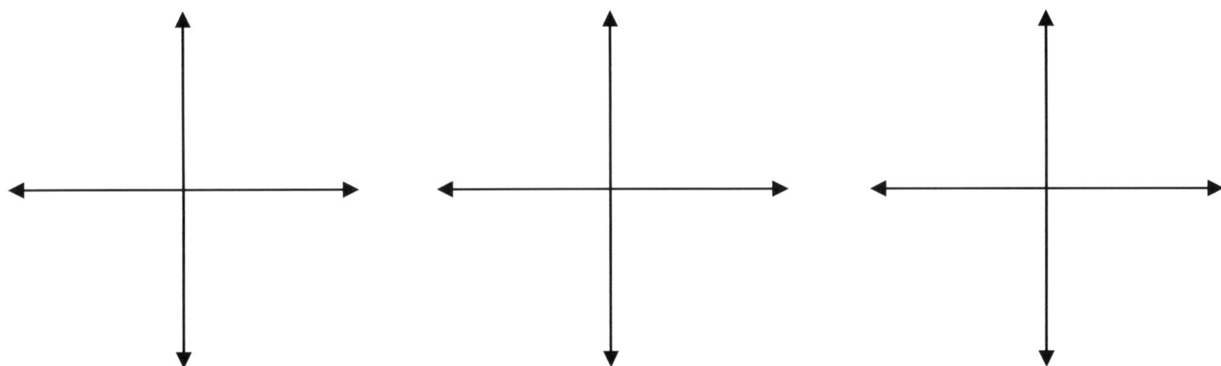

3. Calculate the **gradient** of the following data, giving an appropriate unit.

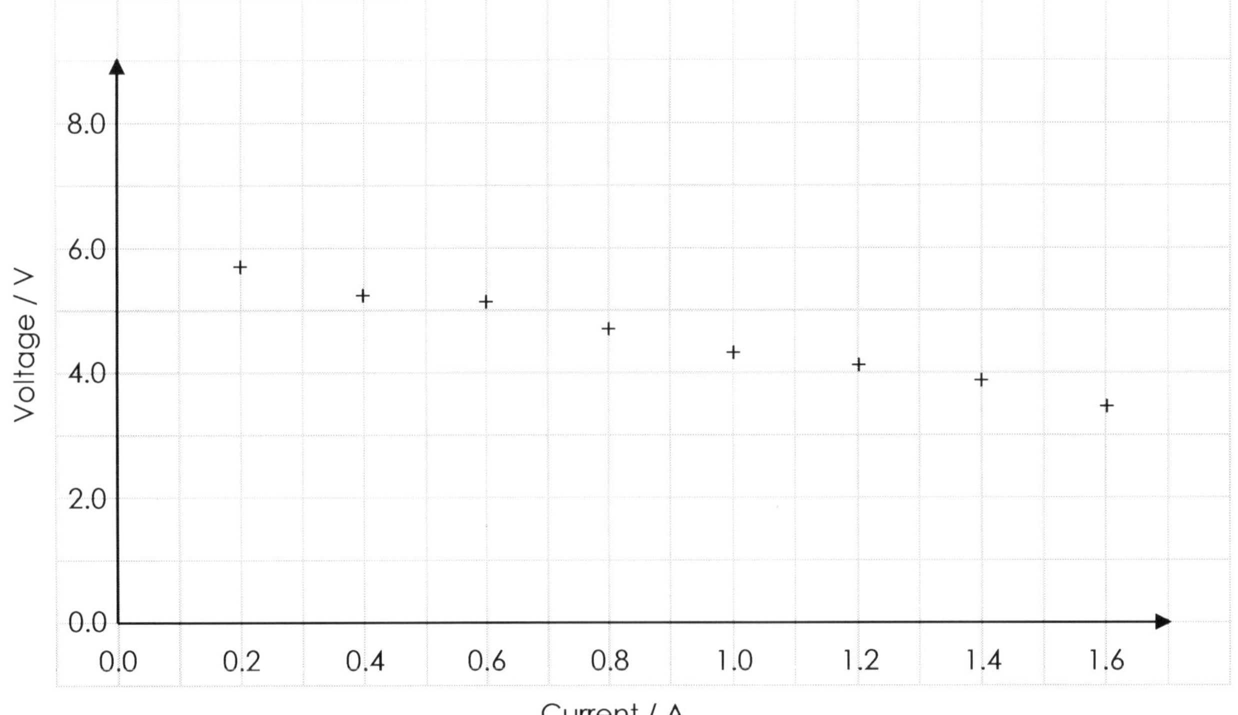

29th September

1 2 3

1. Write down the **units** for:
   a. Upthrust
   b. Elementary charge
   c. Internal resistance
   d. Frequency

2. Calculate the size and direction of the resultant force, using **scale drawing**, produced by vertical forces of 809 N down and 321 N up, and horizontal forces of 1.04 kN left and 432 N to the right.

3. Design and describe a **sensing circuit** used to operate an air conditioning unit. Your circuit should include an NTC thermistor and a fixed resistor.

30th September

1 2 3

1. Calculate the **area** of a circle, in m^2, with a:
   a. Diameter of 520 mm
   b. Radius of 0.67 mm
   c. Diameter of 2.3 x 10^9 nm
   d. Radius of 3.14 μm

2. Write the following derived unit in terms of SI Base Units: **watts**

3. Design and describe a **sensing circuit** used to operate a garden light. Your circuit should include an LDR and a fixed resistor.

SEPTEMBER REVIEW

You know the score – reflect on the start of your A Levels.

A Level Physics Content	Red	Amber	Green
I can express some derived units in their **base units**.			
I can recall electrical **circuit symbols**.			
I can calculate the equation for a **straight line**.			
I can apply the equation for **resistors** in **parallel**.			
I can add vectors using **scale drawing**.			
I can add vectors using **mathematical** methods.			

Any other comments:

OCTOBER

OCTOBER

Managing your workload at A Level is very different from GCSE. You will have a lot more study time outside of lessons, therefore you will need to plan and organise how you best spend this time learning effectively.

Keep up the effort made so far. You should feel your confidence building and skills developing as you complete more of these daily workout questions.

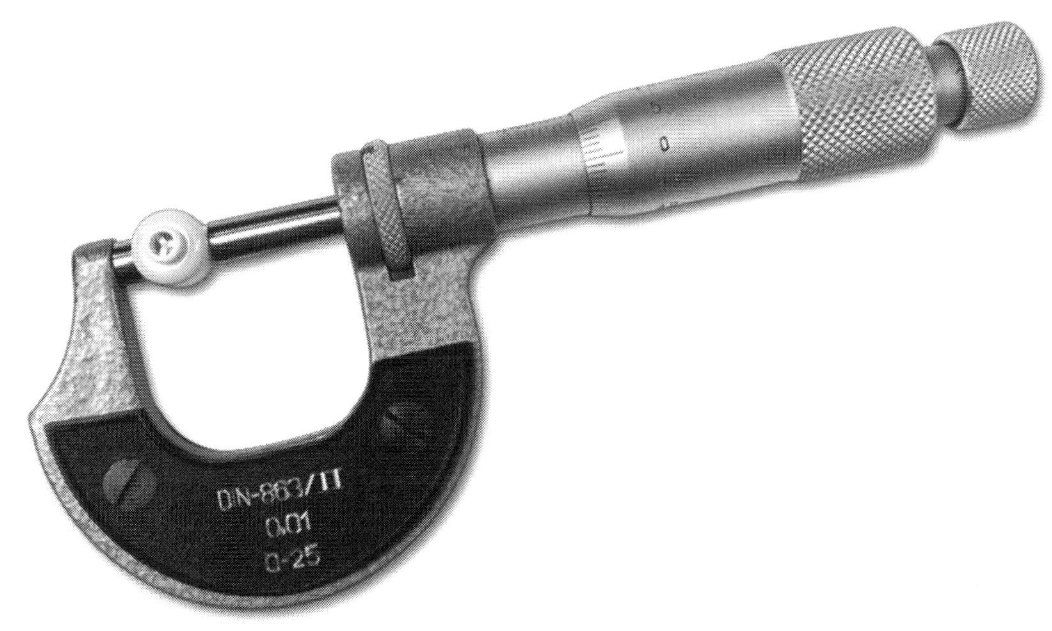

1st October

1 2 3

1. Calculate the **diameter**, in m, of a:
   a. Circle with an area of 1.0 m^2
   b. Sphere with a surface area of 1.0 m^2
   c. Sphere with a volume of 1.0 m^3

2. Read the **quantity** measured in the following diagrams of vernier scales.

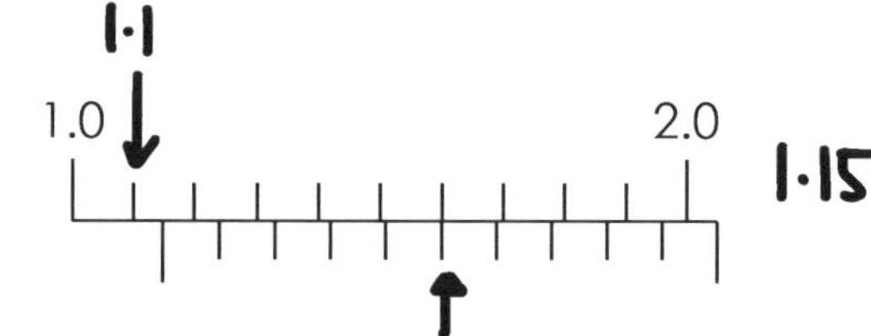

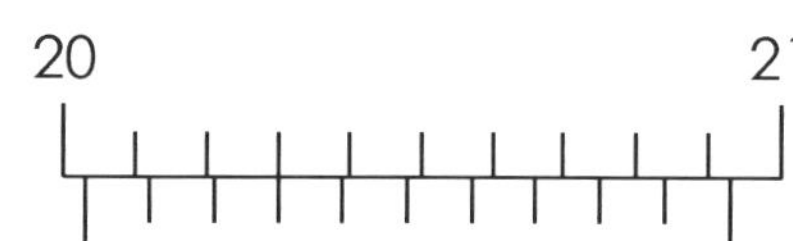

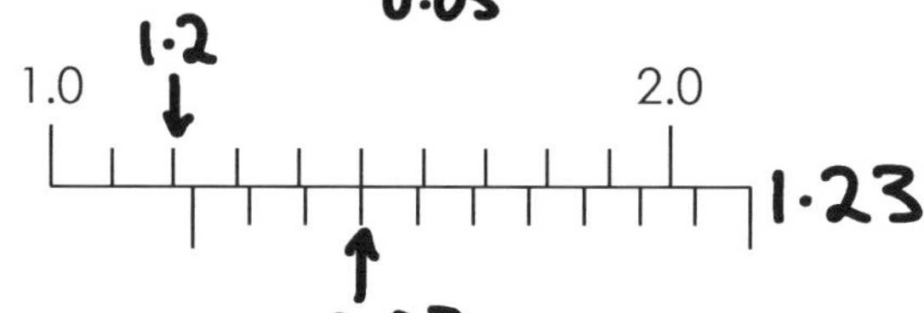

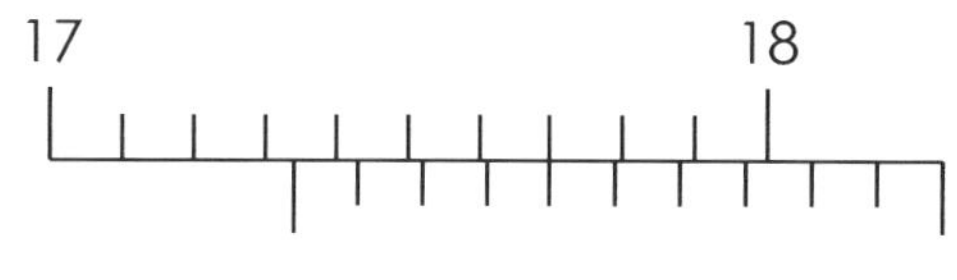

3. Calculate the **current** if 1.0 x 10^{-2} moles of electrons pass a point in 1.0 hour.

2nd October

1. Write down the **mass** in kg, to 4 sf, of:
    a. An electron
    b. A proton
    c. A neutron
    d. An alpha particle

2. Read the **quantity** measured in the following diagrams.

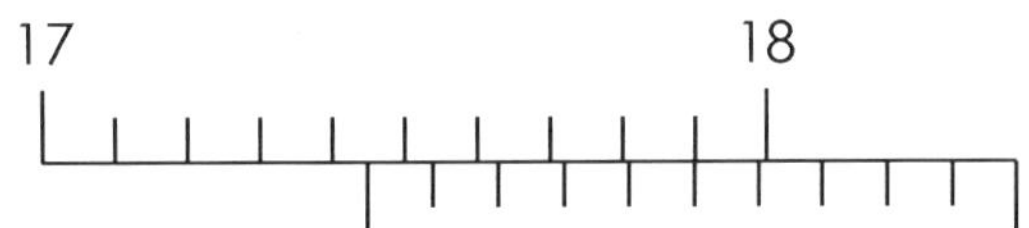

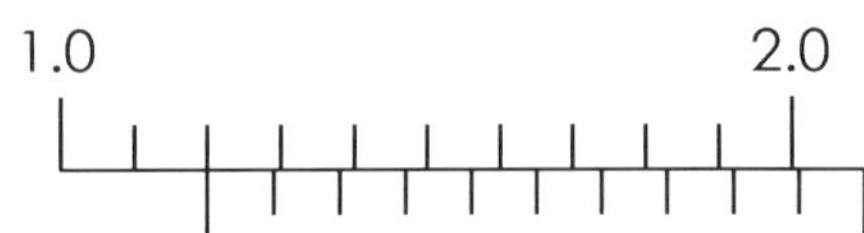

3. Describe the differences between two waves propagated on two strings with the same wavelength and amplitude but one is **stationary** (also called a standing wave) and the other is **progressive**.

3rd October

1 2 3

1. Rearrange the following to make **d** the subject:
   a. $E = V / d$
   b. $A = \pi d^2 / 4$
   c. $n\lambda = d\sin\theta$

2. Read the **quantity** measured in the following diagrams.

3. Calculate the **refractive index** of a material if light travels at 2.6×10^8 m s^{-1} through it.

4th October

1 2 3

1. Rearrange the following to make **M** the subject:
   a. $V_g = -GM / r$
   b. $g = -GM / r^2$
   c. $F = -GMm / r^2$

2. Read the **quantity** measured in the following diagrams.

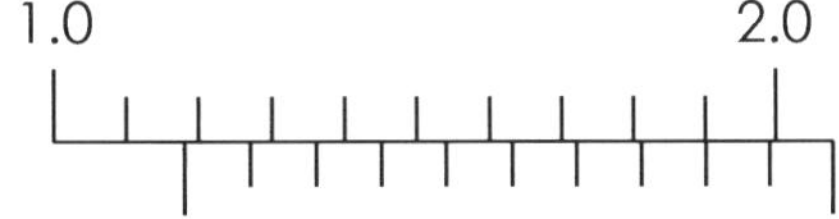

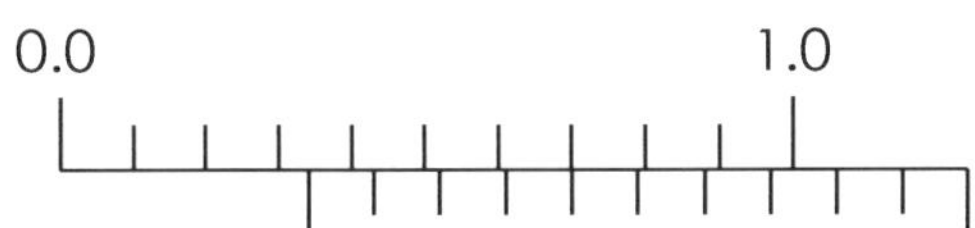

3. An artillery gun of mass 1860 kg is initially at rest. It fires a shell of mass 14.9 kg with a muzzle velocity of 708 m s^{-1}. Calculate the **recoil velocity** of the gun.

5th October

1 2 3

1. Write the following distances in **standard form** to **3 significant** figures – and find out what they represent.

   a. 149 597 871 000 m

   b. 30 856 775 800 000 000 m

   c. 9 460 730 473 000 000 m

2. Read the **quantity** measured in the following diagrams.

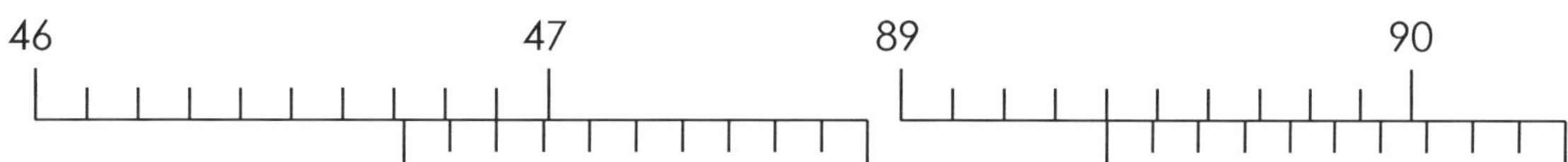

3. Explain why **electricity** is transmitted at very high AC voltages in overhead cables across the country.

6th October

1 2 3

1. Write the following quantities in **standard form** to **3 significant** figures – and find out what they represent.

    a. 6 378 100 m

    b. 5 972 200 000 000 000 000 000 000 kg

    c. 1 988 470 000 000 000 000 000 000 000 000 kg

2. A ball bearing is released from a height of 1.62 m. Calculate how **long** it will take to reach the ground.

3. The block is at **rest** on a slope. Calculate the size of the **friction** acting up the slope if the block's weight is 10 N and θ = 38˚.

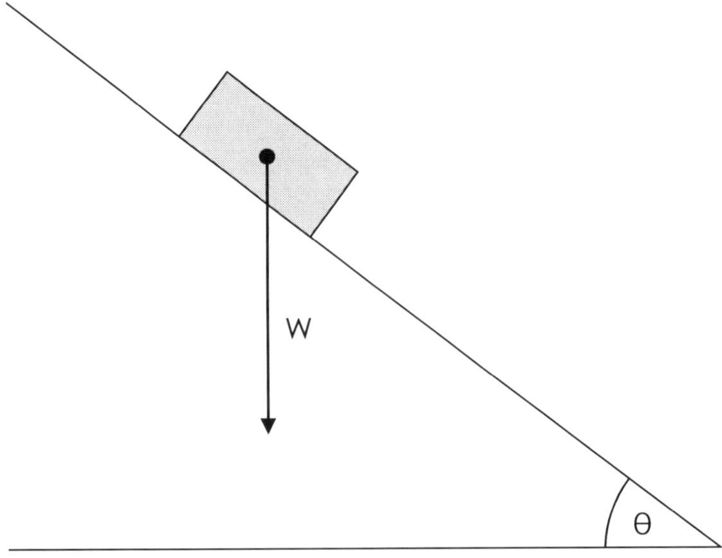

7th October

1 2 3

1. Calculate the **mean**, **mode** and **median** of the following set of numbers:

   102, 103, 100, 99, 91, 111, 104, 102, 104, 104

2. A ball bearing is released from a height of 1.62 m. Calculate its **velocity** as it reaches the ground.

3. The block is **sliding** down the slope at a constant velocity. Calculate the size of the **friction** acting up the slope if the block's weight is 10 N and θ = 38°.

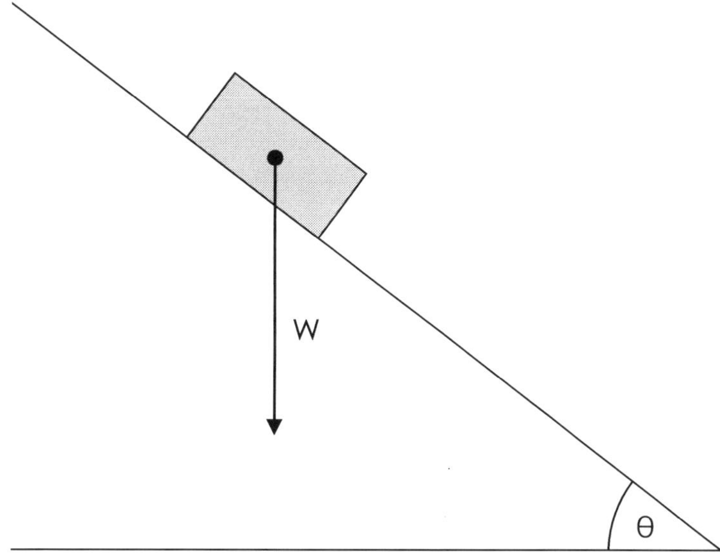

8th October (part 1)

1. Draw an appropriate **line of best fit** for the following graphs.

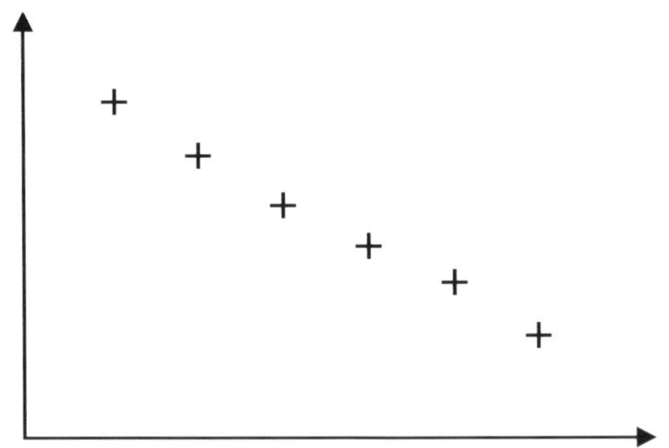
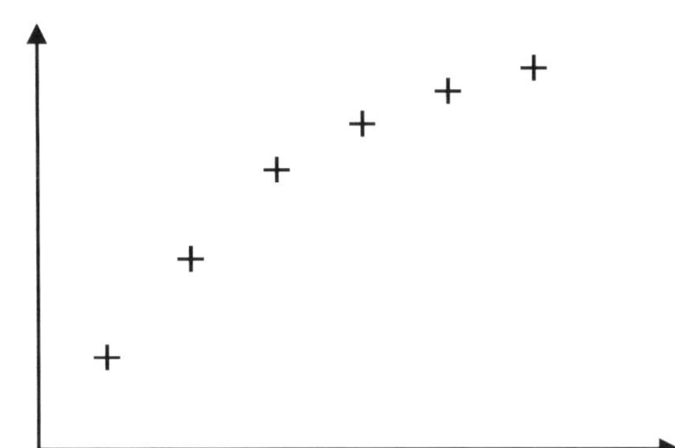
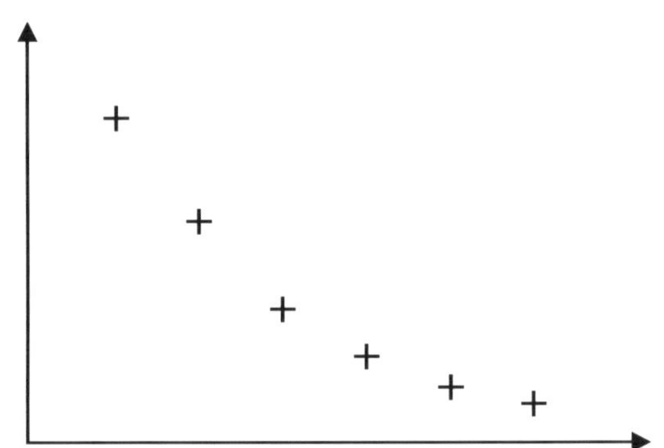
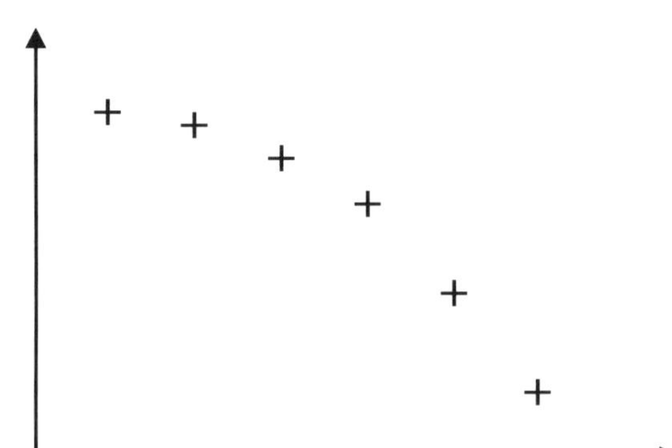

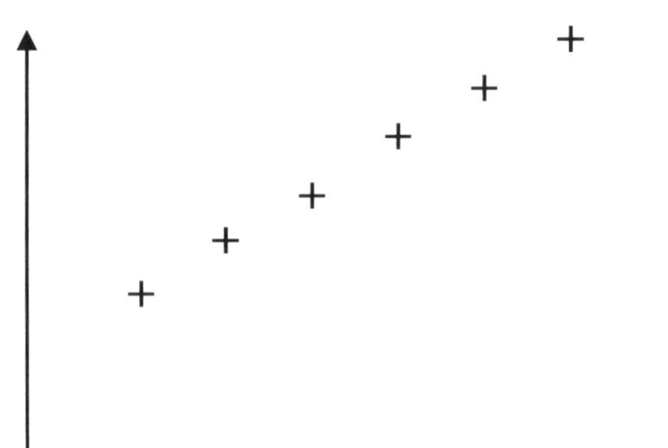

8th October (part 2)

2

2. Sketch a **sinusoidal** curve for the following graphs:

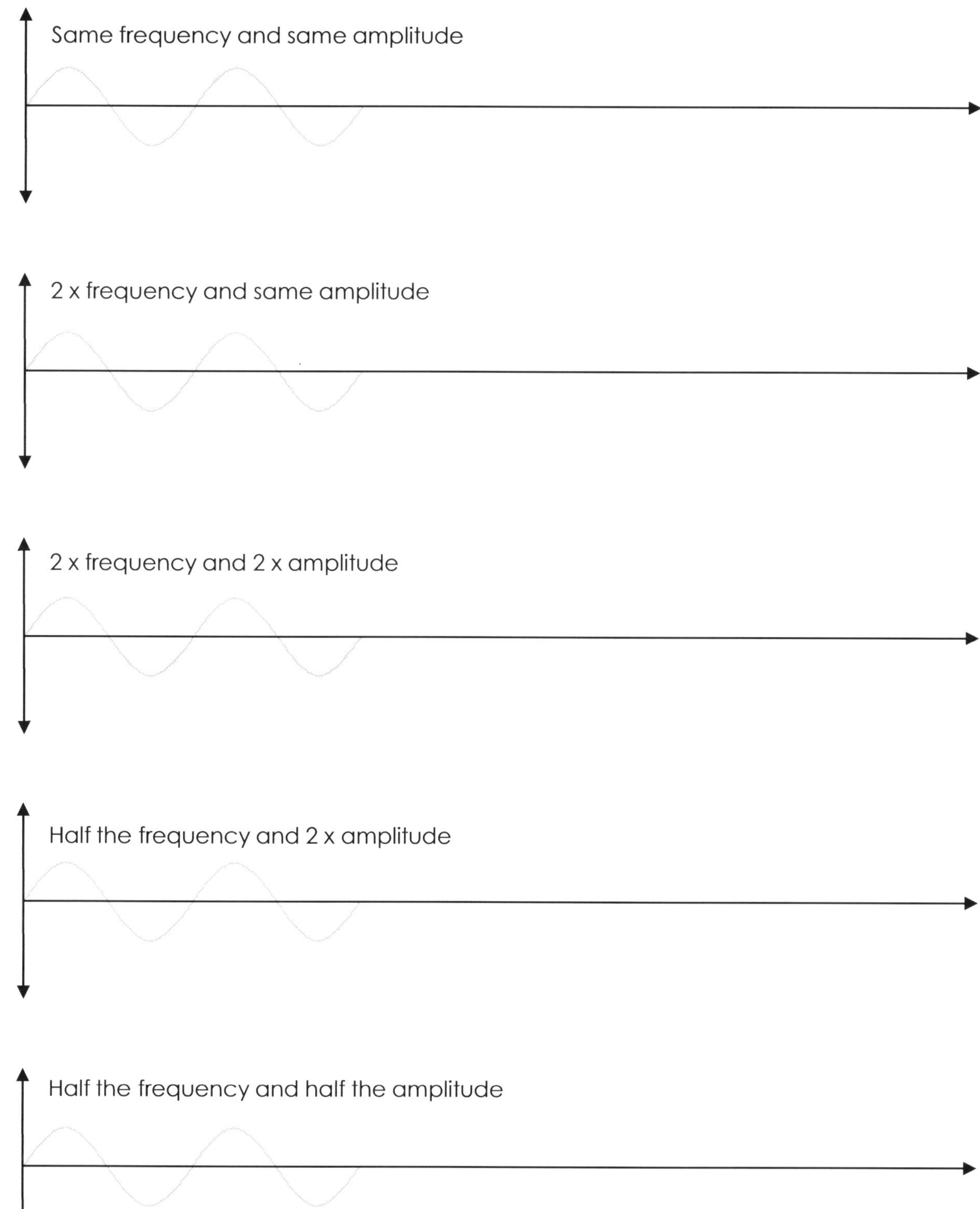

9th October

1 2 3

1. Calculate the **surface area**, in m^2, of a sphere with a diameter of:
   a. 2.00 m
   b. 1.00 m
   c. 0.50 m
   d. 0.25 m

2. Describe what is meant by **accuracy**.

3. Briefly describe how you would investigate the **IV characteristics** of a **resistor**. Include a suitable circuit diagram, measurements recorded and how uncertainties would be reduced.

Make sure you order your copy of the next book ready for November!

10th October

1 2 3

1. Calculate the **volume**, in m^3, of a sphere with a radius of:
   a. 6.37×10^3 km
   b. 6.96×10^8 m
   c. 0.10 nm
   d. 1.0 fm

2. Describe what is meant by **resolution**.

3. Draw a simple diagram of a **stationary/standing** wave and label the nodes and antinodes:
   a. On a string
   b. In a tube open at one end

11th October

1 2 3

1. Convert the following distances to **metres**:
   a. 3.14×10^4 mm
   b. 31.4×10^{-6} μm
   c. 0.0314×10^6 km
   d. 31.4×10^{14} cm
   e. 3.14×10^{-3} mm

2. Read the **quantity** measured in the following diagrams for a screw gauge micrometer.

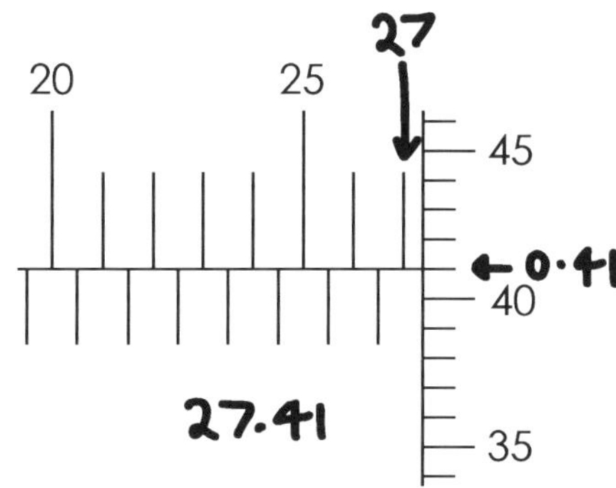

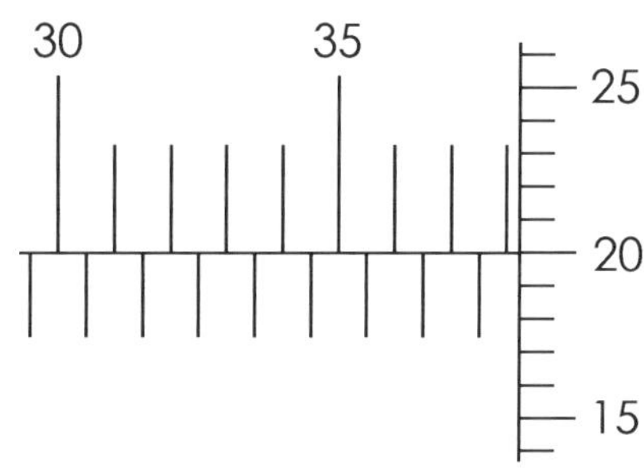

3. When reading any scale in experimental physics, describe what can be done to minimise **parallax error**. Include a description of what parallax error is.

12th October

1 2 3

1. Convert the following distances to **metres**:
   a. 3.14×10^{-4} nm
   b. 314×10^{-6} pm
   c. 0.0314×10^{4} km
   d. 31.4×10^{14} fm
   e. 3140×10^{-8} Mm

2. Read the **quantity** measured in the following diagrams.

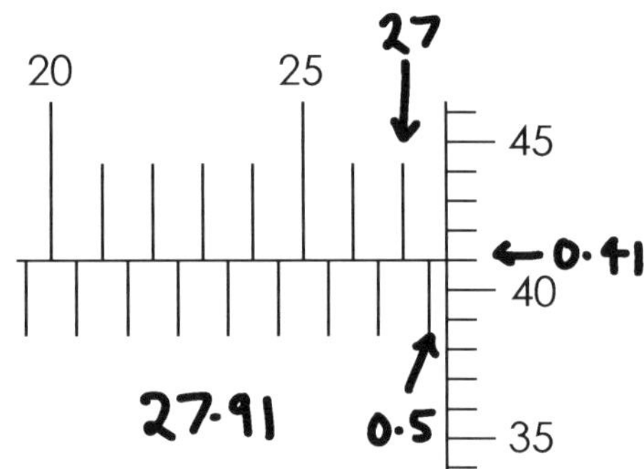

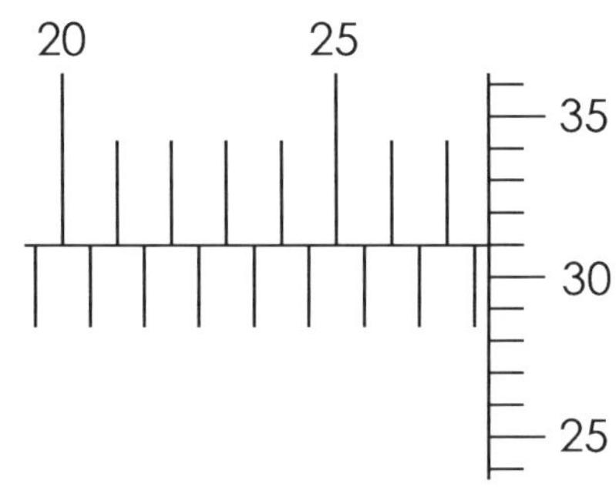

3. Calculate the **gradient** of the following data, giving an appropriate unit.

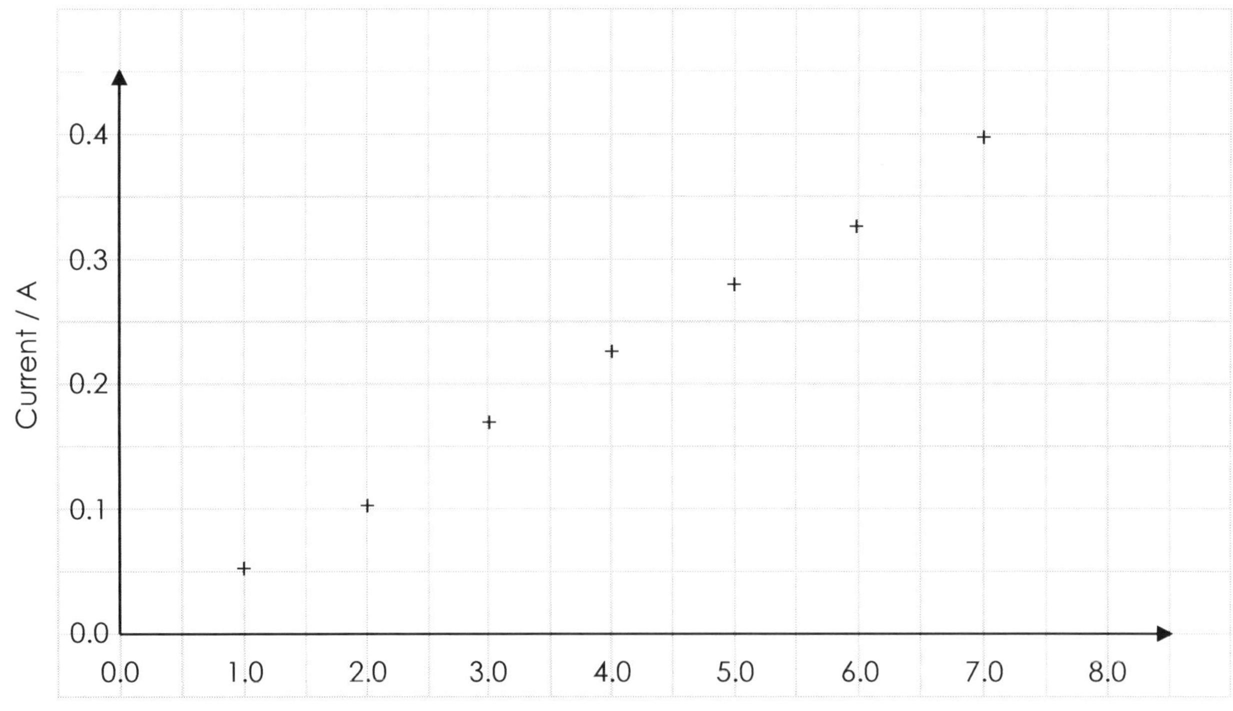

13th October

1 2 3

1. Calculate the length of the hypotenuse of a right-angled triangle if the opposite side to an angle of 28° is 3.6 cm.

2. Read the **quantity** measured in the following diagrams.

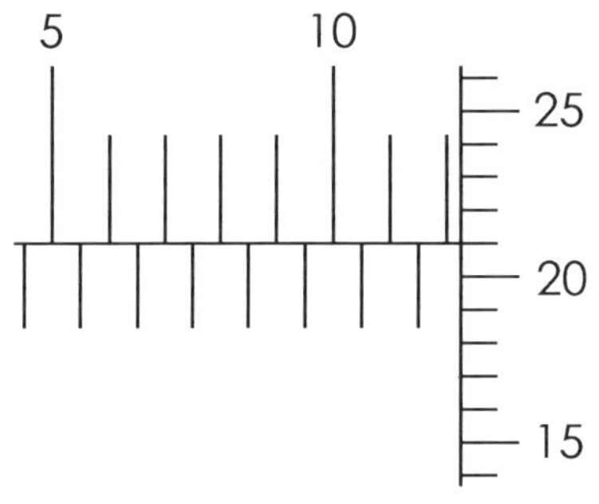

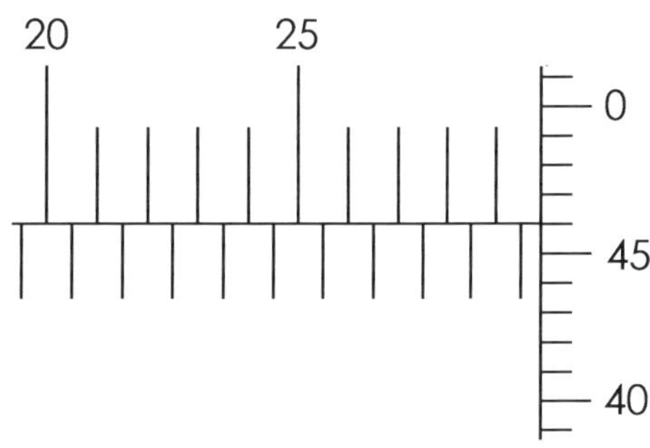

3. Calculate the **gradient** of the following data, giving an appropriate unit.

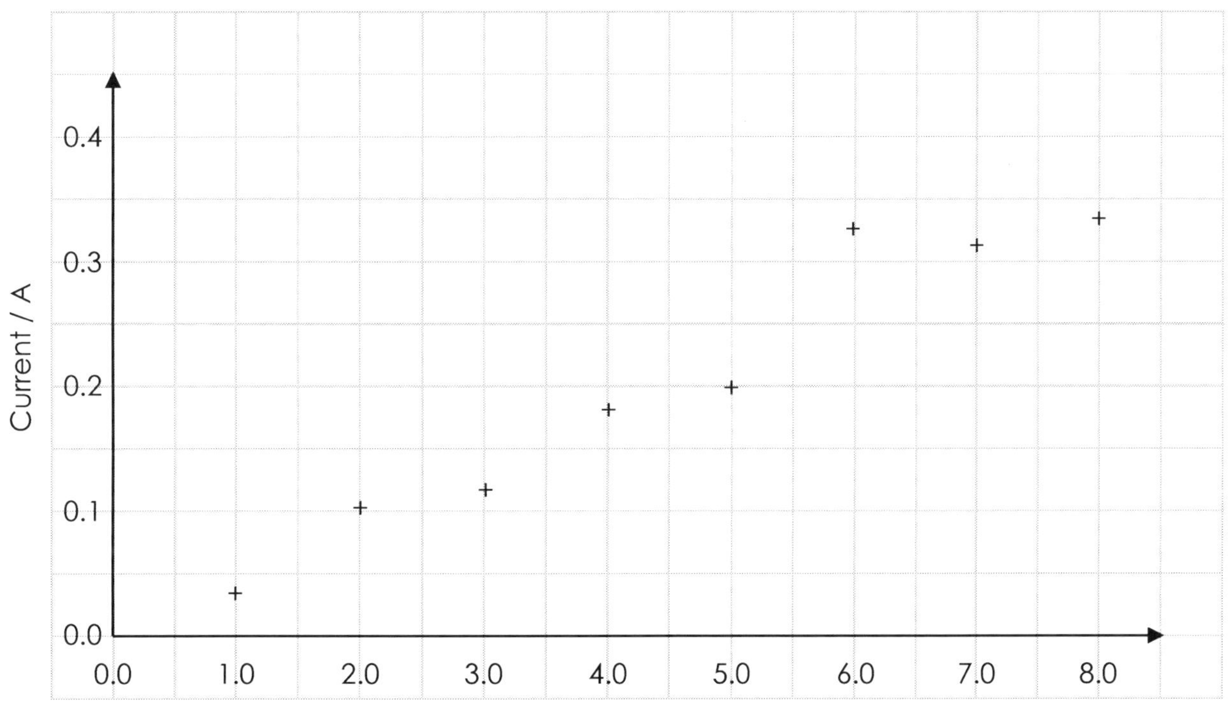

14th October

1 2 3

1. Calculate the length of the hypotenuse of a right-angled triangle if the adjacent side to an angle of 18° is 7.8 cm.

2. Read the **quantity** measured in the following diagrams.

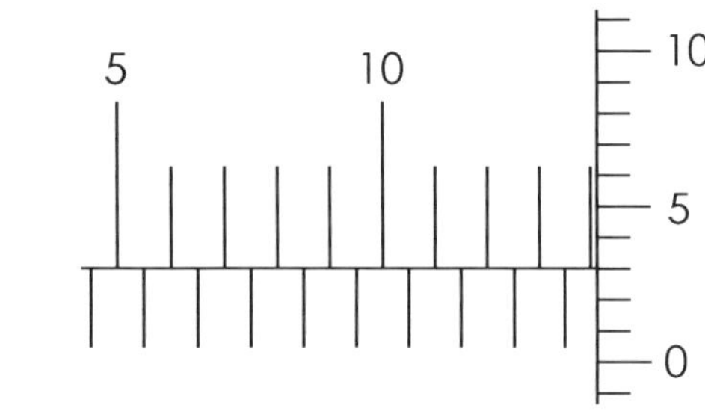

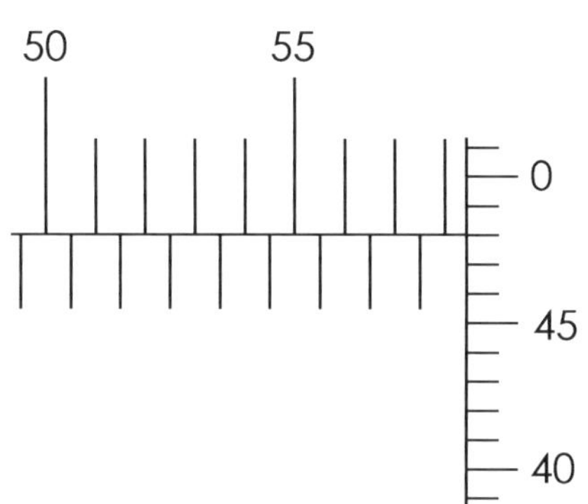

3. Describe and explain how the **resistance** of a wire changes with temperature.

15th October

1 2 3

1. Calculate **sinθ** and **cosθ** for the following values of θ (to 2 d.p.).
   a. 23°
   b. 67°
   c. 34°
   d. 56°
   e. 45°

2. Read the **quantity** measured in the following diagrams.

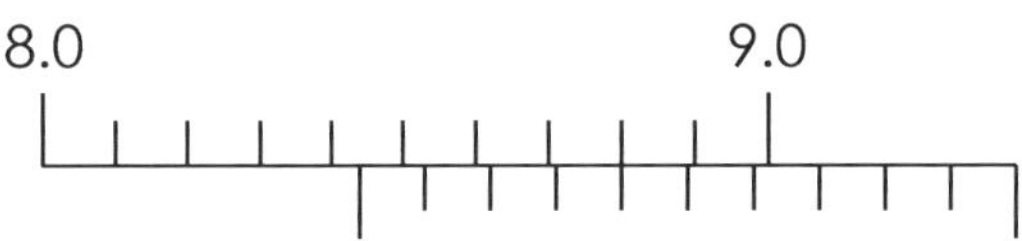

3. Sketch the **standing** wave formed on a string fixed at both ends:
   a. First harmonic

   b. Second harmonic

   c. Third harmonic

   d. Fourth harmonic

16th October

1 2 3

1. Write the following numbers in **standard form** to **3 significant** figures:

   a. 3 600 s

   b. 86 400 s

   c. 31 556 557 s

2. State and explain the effect of **Kirchhoff's 1st law** (the current law).

3. A student takes the following repeated readings of potential difference at a certain current and resistance.

   Calculate the **value** that should be quoted for the voltage, including the **absolute uncertainty** in this measured value.

Voltage / V
9.22
9.83
9.25
9.17
9.20
9.16

17th October

1 2 3

1. Convert the following volumes into **m³**:
   a. 1.0 cm^3
   b. 1.0 mm^3
   c. 568 ml
   d. 22.4 ltr

2. State and explain the effect of **Kirchhoff's 2nd law** (the voltage law).

3. In an investigation to calculate the resistance of a wire, a student measures the voltage as 12.03 ± 0.05 V and the current as 0.25 ± 0.01 A.

   Calculate the value that should be given for the resistance, including the **percentage uncertainty**.

18th October

1 2 3

1. Convert the following distances into **m**:
   a. 1.609 km
   b. 630 nm
   c. 0.833 femtometres
   d. A light-year

2. Rearrange $f = \frac{1}{2L}\sqrt{\frac{T}{\mu}}$ to make:
   a. **L** the subject
   b. **T** the subject
   c. **μ** the subject

3. State the laboratory equipment required to measure the **specific heat capacity** of water. Include a circuit diagram and how significant sources of error can be minimised.

19th October

1 2 3

1. Convert the following masses into **kg**:
   a. 1 tonne
   b. 240 g
   c. 3 560 mg
   d. 937.4×10^{-7} Mg

2. Describe what is meant by a '**force multiplier**' and how we can multiply a force without violating the law of conservation of energy.

3. Describe in detail, in terms of **forces**, what happens to a skydiver between the moment they jump out of a plane and the moment they reach terminal velocity.

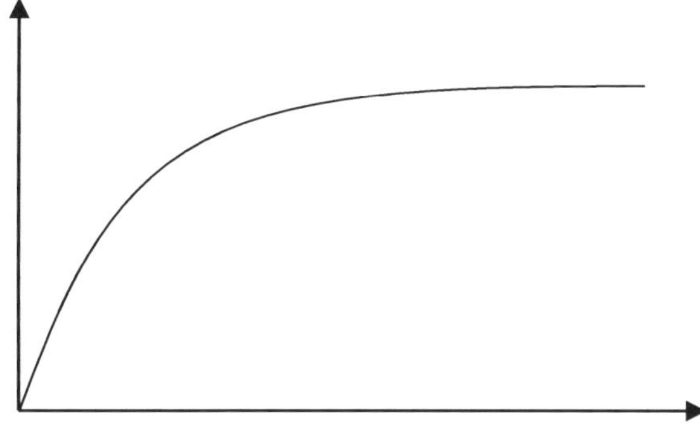

20th October

1 2 3

1. Write down the **units** for:
   a. Momentum
   b. Resistivity
   c. Electromotive force
   d. Mass per unit length

2. State the **masses** (in kg), **charges** (in C) and **penetrating** ability of alpha, beta minus and gamma radiation.

3. Describe in detail, in terms of forces, what happens to a skydiver travelling at **terminal velocity** between the moment they release their parachute and the moment they reach terminal velocity again.

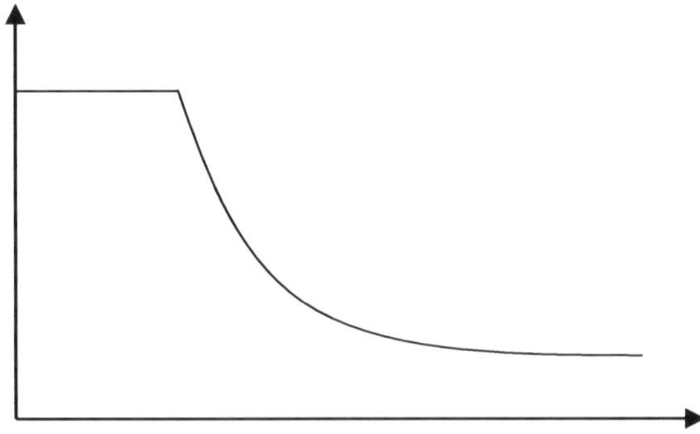

21st October

1 2 3

1. Calculate the **angle of refraction** of a wave that crosses from air into a transparent material, with a refractive index of 1.3, at an angle of incidence of 24°.

2. Calculate the **moment** of a 24 N force acting at a perpendicular distance, to a pivot, of 30 cm.

3. Calculate the **gradient** and **intercept** of the following data, giving an appropriate unit.

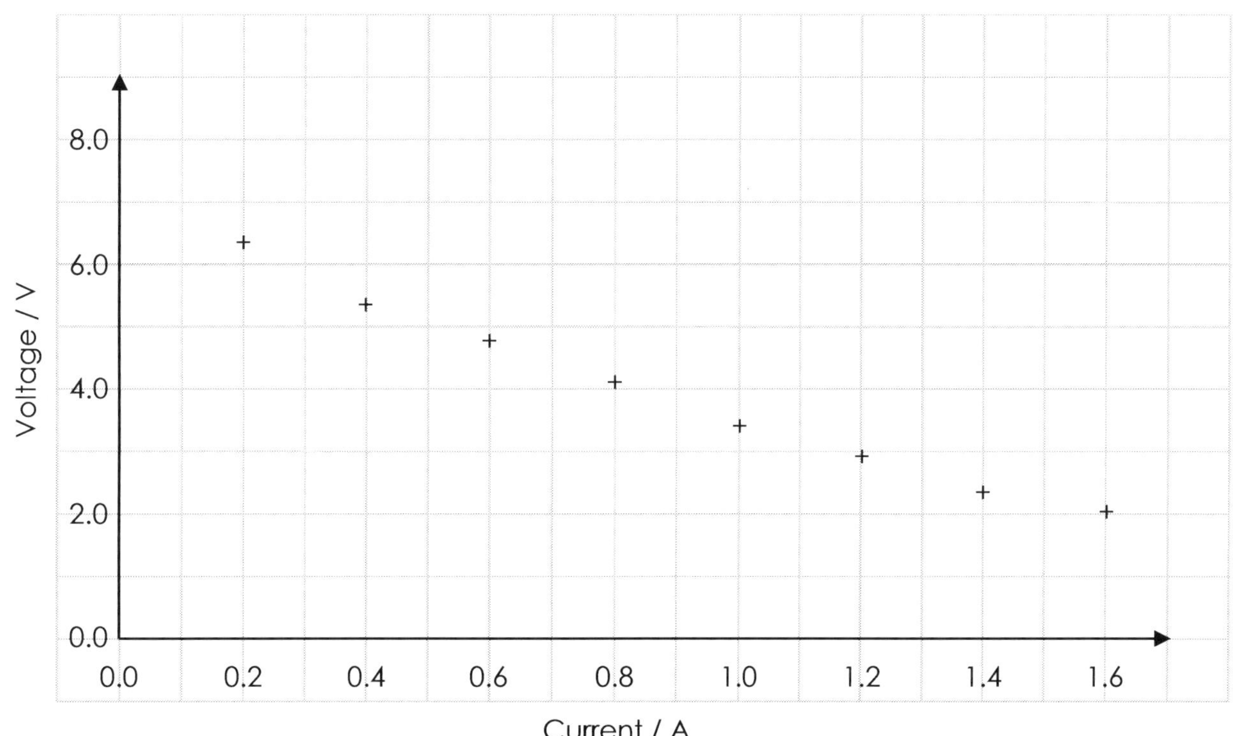

22nd October

1 2 3

1. Write down the charge, in **coulombs**, of:
    a. A positron
    b. An alpha particle
    c. A neutron
    d. An up quark

2. Define the **centre of mass** of an object.

3. Describe what is usually assumed to be the **resistance** of a wire, an ammeter and a voltmeter in any circuit question.

23rd October - Part 1

1

1. Draw a **tangent** and calculate the **gradient** at:
    a. x = 2.5
    b. x = 5.0

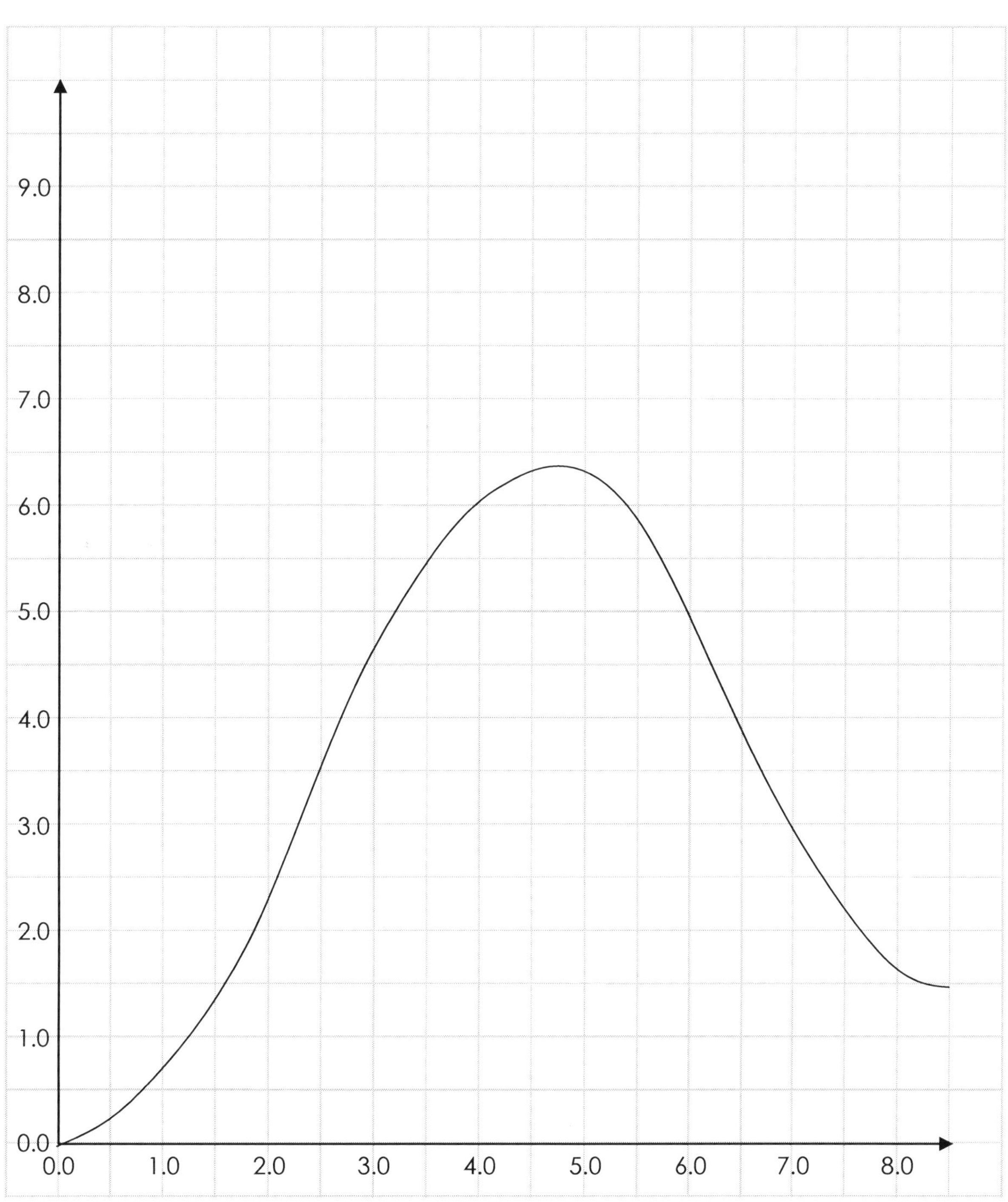

23rd October - Part 2

2. Calculate the **area** under the line between x = 0 and x = 7.0.

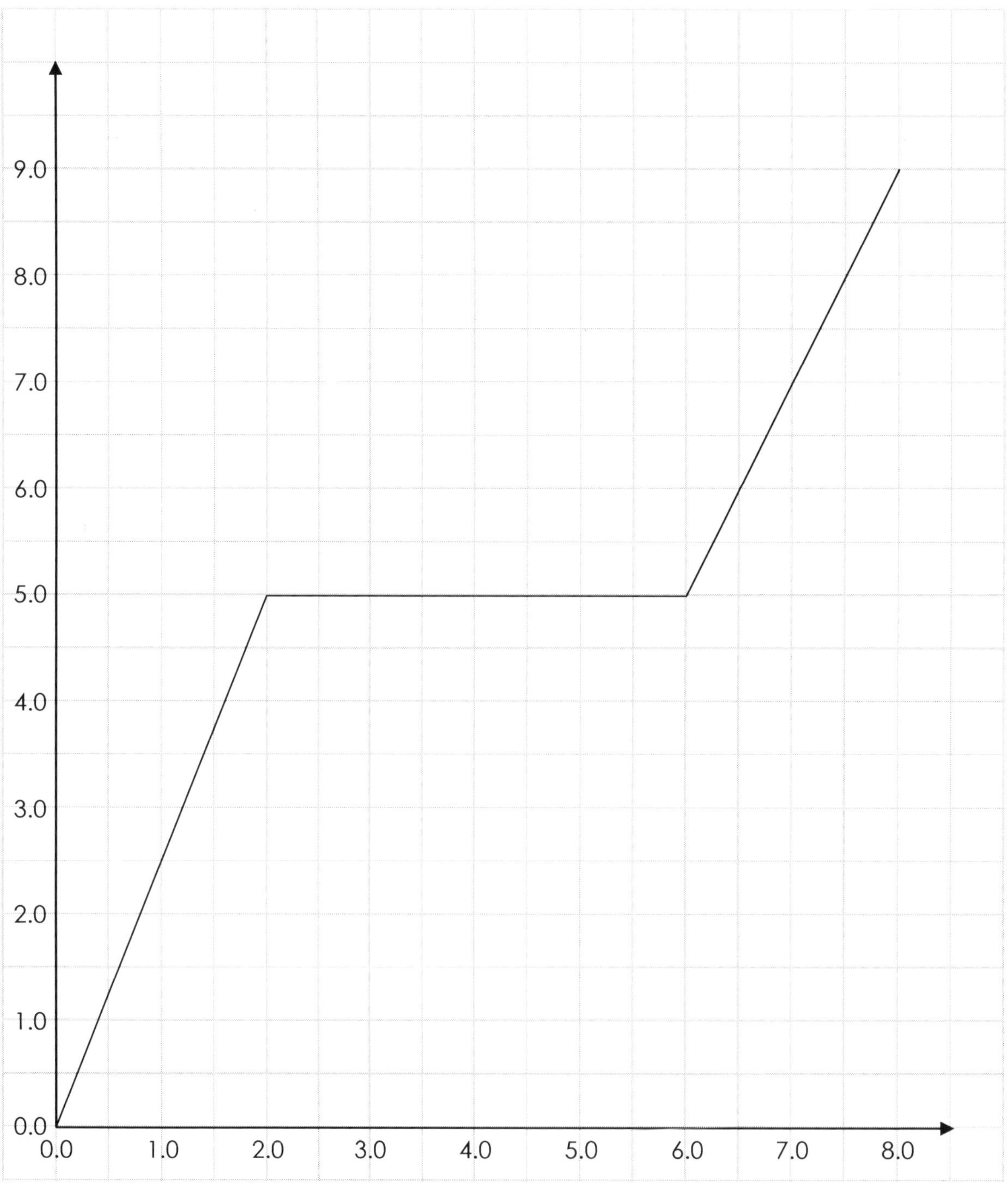

24th October

1 2 3

1. Describe what the area underneath a **force-time** graph represents.

2. In A Level Physics we class waves as either **progressive** or **stationary** (standing). Describe the main difference between the two.

3. A battery has an e.m.f of 9.0 V and an internal resistance of 0.50 Ω. The battery is in series with a bulb of resistance 10 Ω.

   Calculate the **potential difference** across the terminals of the battery.

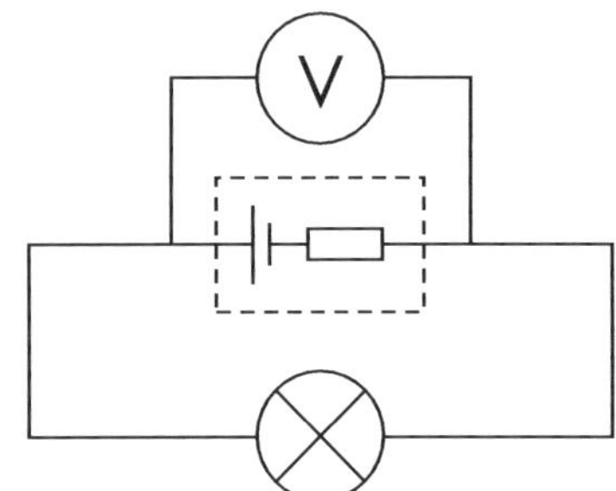

25th October - Part 1

1. Calculate the **acceleration** at:

    a. t = 2.0 s

    b. t = 6.0 s

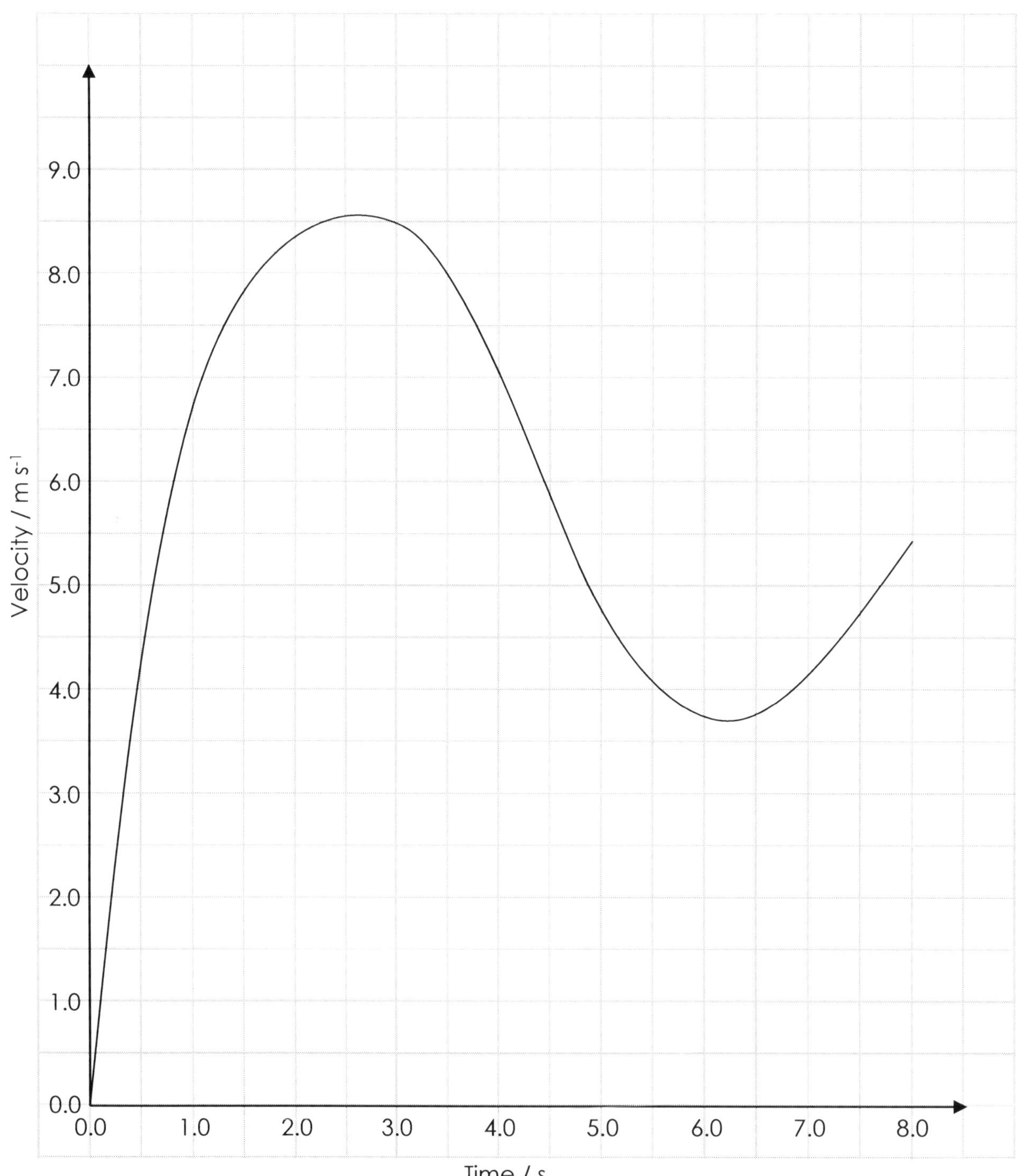

25th October - Part 2

2. Estimate the **displacement** between t = 0.0 and t = 2.5 s.

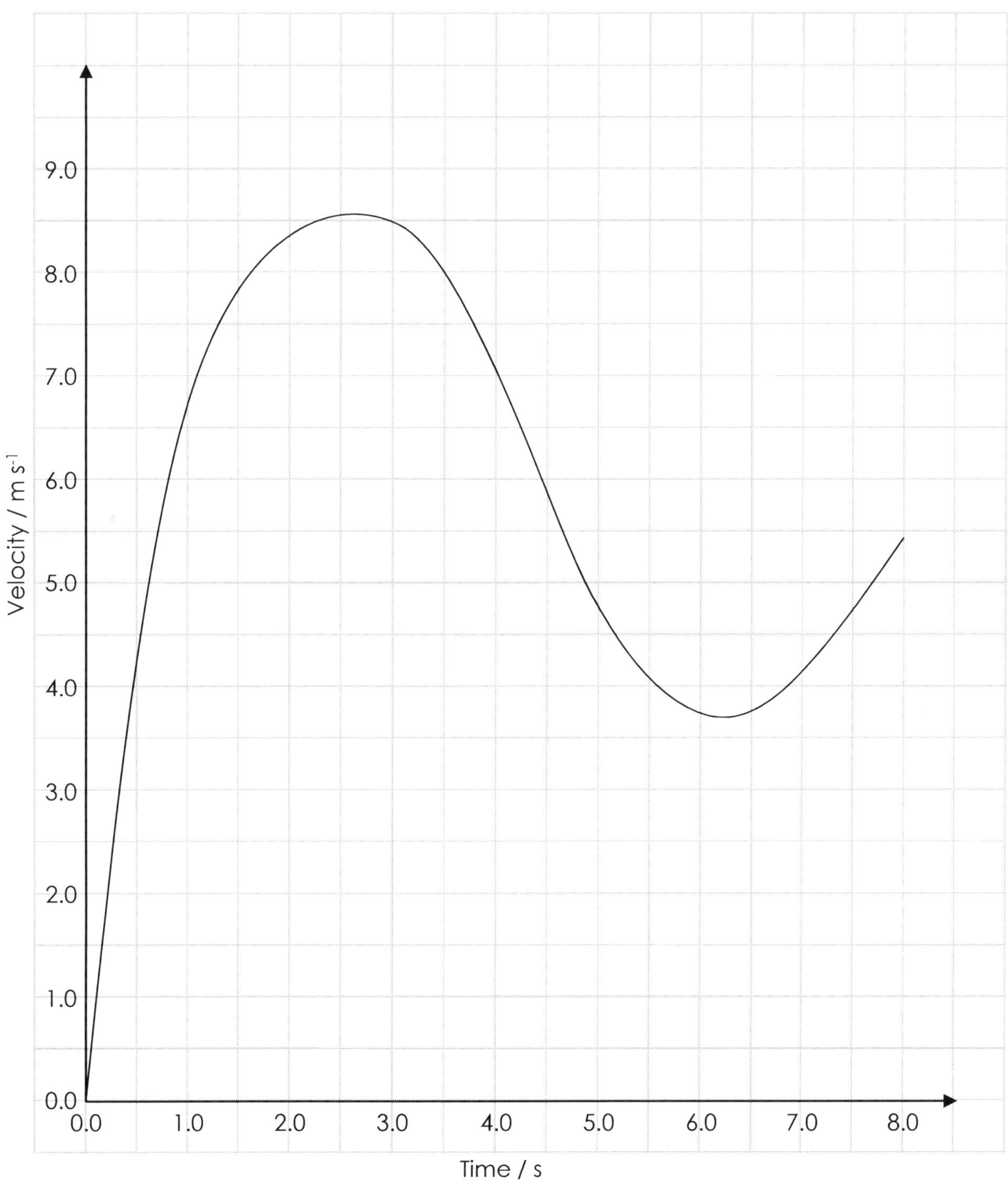

26th October

1 2 3

1. Calculate **tanθ** for the following values of θ (to 2 d.p.).
   a. 0°
   b. 30°
   c. 45°
   d. 60°
   e. 90°
2. Describe what is meant by the terms '**path difference**' and '**phase difference**' for waves.
3. Calculate the **refractive index** of the semi-circular block.

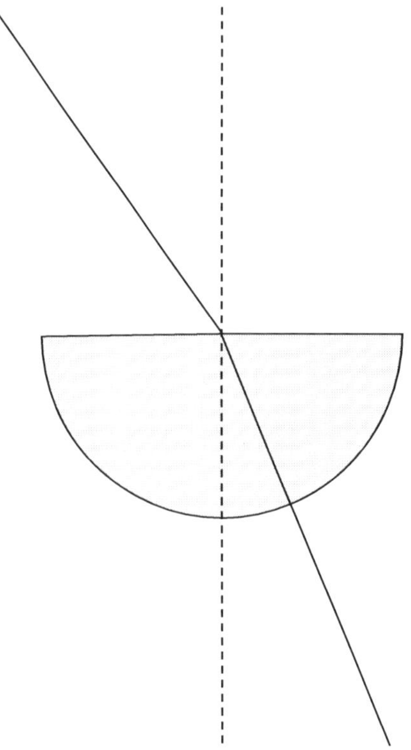

27th October

1 2 3

1. Convert the following angles from degrees to **radians**. Give your answer to 2 d.p.
   a. 0˚
   b. 30˚
   c. 45˚
   d. 60˚
   e. 90˚

2. Describe how you could find the **centre of mass** of a **regular** 2D shape.

3. Work out the **time of flight** for a javelin thrown with a vertical component of velocity of 20 m s^{-1}. Ignore air resistance.

28th October

1 2 3

1. Convert the following angles from degrees to **radians**. Give your answer to 2 d.p.
   a. 5°
   b. 57°
   c. 82°
   d. 172°
   e. 326°

2. Describe a **practical investigation** you could carry out in order to find the **centre of mass** of an **irregular** 2D shape.

3. Three resistors, of resistances 10 Ω, 20 Ω and 30 Ω, are connected in a circuit. Two are connected in series and one is in parallel.

   Calculate the **greatest** resistance and the **least** resistance possible.

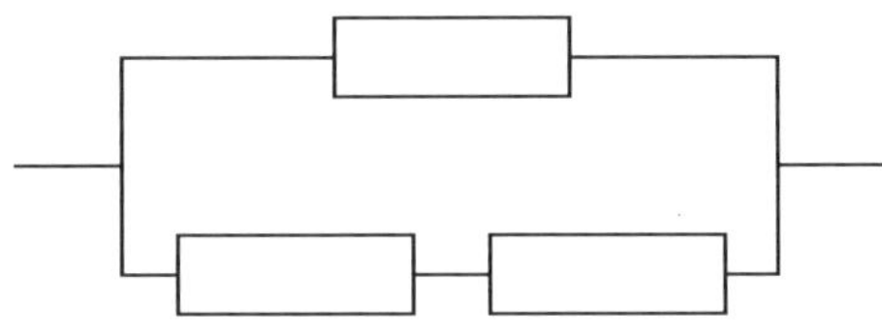

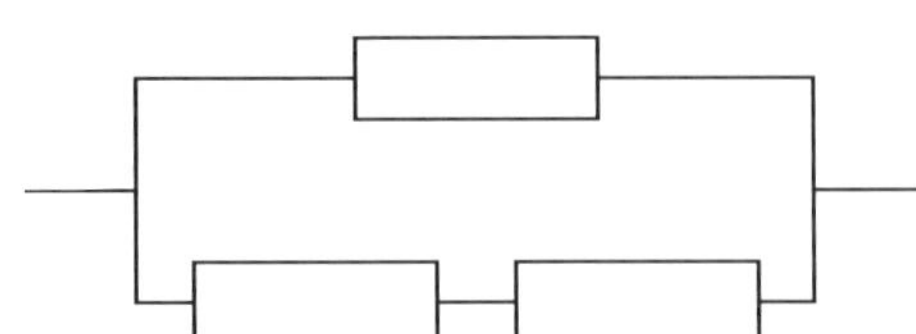

29th October

1

1. Estimate the **displacement** during the first 8.0 s.

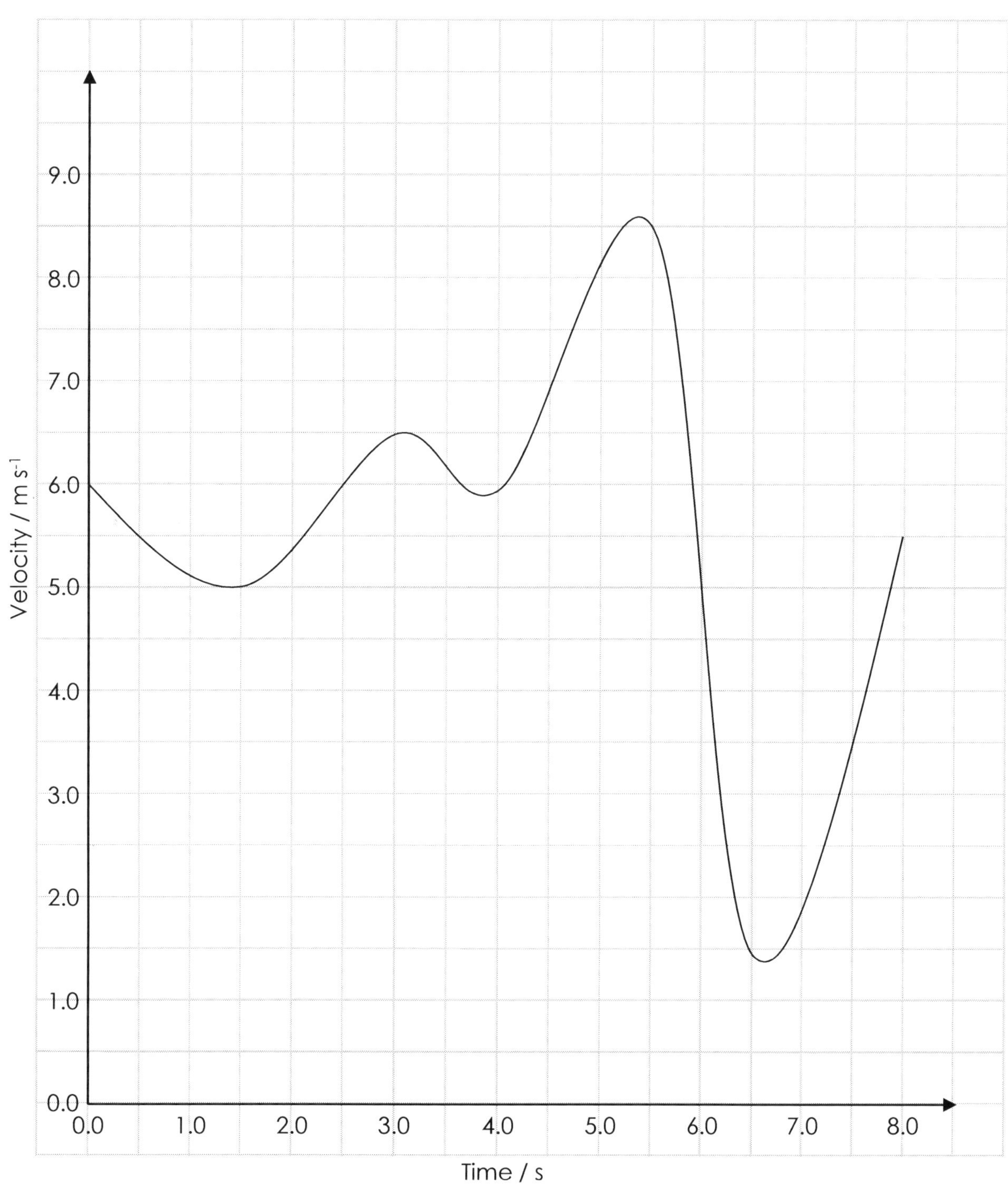

30th October

1 2 3

1. Draw a beautiful freehand **sine** curve.

2. The efficiency of a hairdryer is 87%. It is connected to a 230 V supply and draws a current of 1.0 A.

   Calculate the **output power** of the hairdryer.

3. A cell of e.m.f 12.0 V is in series with an LDR of resistance 13.2 Ω and a variable resistor set to 18.7 Ω.

   Draw a circuit diagram and calculate the **potential difference** across the LDR. Assume the cell has negligible internal resistance.

31st October

1 2 3

1. A 0.200 m^3 block of copper is extruded into a wire of diameter 0.90 mm. Calculate how **long** it is.

2. The efficiency of a bouncy ball is 0.58. It is dropped from a height of 1.00 m. Calculate the **height** the ball reaches after 7 bounces.

3. Define **critical angle** and calculate the critical angle for a glass block with n = 1.4.

OCTOBER REVIEW

Well done! Have a look through this workbook to see how many questions you have now completed – it's a LOT of work.

This is a great start to your A Level Physics and a solid foundation on which the rest of the course is built.

Now onto Book 2…

A Level Physics Content	Red	Amber	Green
I can read a **vernier** scale.			
I can calculate **refractive index**.			
I can resolve forces **perpendicular** and **parallel** to a **slope**.			
I can sketch a **standing wave**.			
I can calculate a **gradient** with an appropriate unit.			
I can estimate the **area** under a graph and identify what this represents.			
Any other comments:			

ANSWERS

ANSWERS

Check your work with the short answers in the back of this book.

To find full worked solutions and video support head over to:

ALevelPhysicsOnline.com/**book-1**

1st July

1. 53.1°
2. $E_k \propto m$
3. E_k = 540 000 J p = 36 000 kg m s^{-1}

2nd July

1. 3.7 m
2. $F \propto a$
3. Magnitude and direction. Velocity, force and weight.

3rd July

1. The sum of the squares of the two side lengths of a right-angled triangle is equal to the square of the hypotenuse: $a^2 + b^2 = c^2$
2. $f \propto 1/T$
3. 127 Hz

4th July

1. 5.2 cm
2. $a \propto 1/m$
3. 2.5 A

5th July

1. 7.1 cm
2. $p \propto v$
3. Central dense nucleus containing positively charged protons and neutral neutrons. This is where most of the mass is. Orbiting the nucleus are negatively charged electrons in shells.

6th July

1. 13 m
2. $E_k \propto v^2$
3. Electric current is the flow of negatively charged electrons. Conventional current is from the positive terminal to the negative terminal in a DC circuit.

7th July

1. a. 8.99×10^9

   b. 2.9979×10^8

   c. 9.6485×10^4
2. a. 0.707 b. 0.707

   c. 0.707 d. 0.707
3. 960 m

8th July

1. a. 2.898×10^{-3}

   b. 9.1094×10^{-31}

   c. 5.670×10^{-8}
2. a. 0.500 b. 0.500

   c. 0.866 d. 0.866
3. 3.0×10^8 m s^{-1}

9th July

1. a. -1.60×10^{-19} C

   b. 0 C

   c. $+1.60 \times 10^{-19}$ C
2. $u = v - at$
3. 0.667 m s^{-2}

10th July

1. a. 8.0×10^{11}

   b. 8.0×10^{11}

   c. 9.0×10^{11}

   d. 1.2×10^{12}
2. $u = \sqrt{(v^2 - 2as)}$
3. 180 m s^{-1}

11th July

1. a. 2.0×10^{-3}

   b. 5.0×10^{-4}

   c. 0.50

   d. 5.0×10^2

11th July - continued

2. a. $d = V / E$

   b. $d = n\lambda / \sin\theta$

   c. $d = \sqrt{(4A / \pi)}$
3. -0.23 m s^{-2}

12th July

1. a. 6.0×10^4

   b. 2.4×10^5

   c. 4.2×10^5

   d. 4.8×10^5
2. a. $Q = p / Br$

   b. $Q = W / V$

   c. $Q = F / Bv$
3. 71.4 m

13th July

1. a. -2.0×10^4

   b. 1.6×10^5

   c. -3.8×10^5

   d. -3.2×10^5
2. If the resultant force acting on an object is zero and the object is:
   - stationary, the object remains stationary
   - moving, the object continues to move at the same velocity

   A bird flying at 30 m s^{-1} in a straight line must have no resultant force acting on it.
3. About 6.6 N and 107°

14th July

1. Mean = 5

   Mode = 3

   Median = 3

14th July - continued

2. The resultant force on an object is proportional to the rate of change of momentum.

   Double the force and you get double the acceleration.

3. About 5.8 N

15th July

1. Mean = 45.1

   Mode = 45

   Median = 45

2. The force of object A on object B is equal in magnitude, opposite in direction and of the same type as the force of object B on object A.

   The Earth pulls on you with a force due to gravity. You pull on the Earth with the exact same sized force in the opposite direction.

3. About 10.0 N

16th July

1. a. 6.63×10^{-34}

   b. 1.66×10^{-27}

   c. 8.85×10^{-12}

2. Driving force = drag

   Normal contact force = weight

   No resultant force.

3. 10 N at 37° from vertical

17th July

1. a. 1.67×10^{-27}

   b. 1.67×10^{-27}

   c. 1.38×10^{-23}

   d. 6.67×10^{-11}

2. α m = 4, Q = +2, high

   β m = 1/1830, Q = -1, medium

   γ m = 0, Q = 0, low

3. About 72 N at 56° from vertical

18th July

1. a. 1.6×10^{3}

   b. 1.6×10^{3}

   c. 1.57×10^{3}

   d. 1.6×10^{3}

2. 15 m s^{-1}

3. 1030 N

19th July

1. a. 80

   b. 0.602

   c. 80.0

   d. 1500

2. O = 350 N

   A = 430 N

3. a. Proton – 2 Mass - 4

   b. Proton +1 Mass 0

   c. Proton 0 Mass 0

20th July

1. a. 76

   b. 76

   c. 7.7×10^{3}

   d. 7.660×10^{3}

2. F_H = 87 N

   F_V = 50 N

3. 1.3 m s^{-1}

21st July

1. a. x = -5

   b. x > 2

   c. x < 2

   d. x = ±2

2. F_H = 7.81 kN

   F_V = 22.7 kN

3. 136 m

22nd July

1. One joule of work is done when a force of one newton causes a displacement of one metre.

2. Total displacement

3. 0.60 J s^{-1} (W)

23rd July

1. The frequency of a wave is the number of waves passing a point each second.

2. 9

3. 1800 Ω

24th July

1. Nuclear fission is the splitting of a large and unstable nucleus while nuclear fusion is the joining of two light nuclei to form a heavier nucleus.

2. 16

3. 1100 Hz

25th July

1. a. m = 2 c = 3

   b. m = 3 c = 2

   c. m = 6 c = 3

   d. m = 3 c = 6

2. a. $B = F / IL\sin\theta$

   b. $I = F / BL\sin\theta$

   c. $L = F / BI\sin\theta$

   d. $\theta = \sin^{-1}(F / BIL)$

3. Fe-56 26p 30n 26e

   Fe-54 26p 28n 26e

   Co-59 27p 32n 27e

   Ni-60 28p 32n 28e

26th July

1. a. m = 3 c = 5

   b. m = 2 c = 1

   c. m = 1 c = 3

   d. m = 0.5 c = 4

26th July - continued

2. $r = \sqrt{(Gm / g)}$

3. 0.887 m s^{-2}

27th July

1. a. m = 2 c = 4

   b. m = 0.125 c = 1.5

   c. m = -1 c = 0

   d. m = 2 c = -4

2. $m = -V_g r / G$

3. 65°

28th July

1. m = 2 y = 2x

2. a. $p = mv$

   b. $p = NkT / V$

   c. $p = \sqrt{(2mE_k)}$

3.   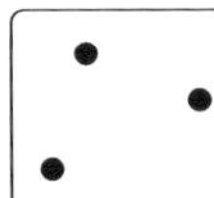

29th July

1. y = 3x - 1

2. $\sin \theta \approx \theta$

   $\cos \theta \approx 1$

   $\tan \theta \approx \theta$

3. 30 m

30th July

1.

3

1

2. The half-life of a radioactive isotope is the time it takes for the number of nuclei of the isotope in a sample to halve or the time it takes for the count-rate, or activity, from a sample containing the radioactive isotope to fall to half its initial level.

3. -2.8 m s^{-2}

31st July

1. 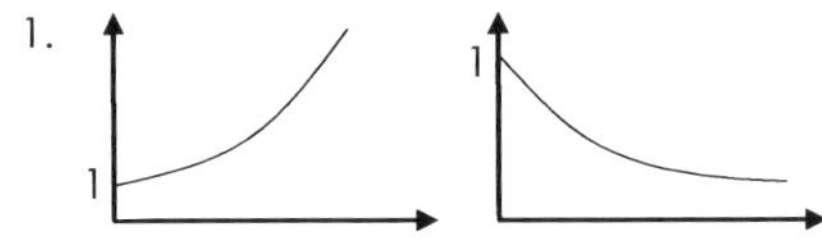

2. Resistance is defined as the ratio of the potential difference across a component to the current through it.

3. $^{238}_{92}\text{U} \rightarrow {}^{234}_{90}\text{Th} + {}^{4}_{2}\text{He}$

   $^{234}_{90}\text{Th} \rightarrow {}^{234}_{91}\text{Pa} + {}^{0}_{-1}\beta$

   $^{234}_{91}\text{Pa} \rightarrow {}^{234}_{92}\text{U} + {}^{0}_{-1}\beta$

1st August

1. a. 13 m^2

   b. 50 m^2

   c. 5.0 x 10^{-3} m^2

   d. 5.0 x 10^{-5} m^2

2. About 8.9 kN at 80° from vertical

3. kg, m, s, A, K, mol and cd

2nd August

1. a. 7.9 x 10^{-5} m^2

   b. 2.0 x 10^{-5} m^2

   c. 7.9 x 10^{-5} m^2

   d. 8.0 x 10^{-6} m^2

2. a. Gravitational constant

   b. Permittivity of free space

   c. Parsec (distance)

   d. Planck's constant

   e. Electronvolt (unit of energy)

   f. Mass of an electron

3. Find a worked solution on website

3rd August

1. a. 0.020 m^2

   b. 0.032 m^2

   c. 0.0205 m^2

2. About 6.1 kN at 53° from vertical

3. F_H = 9.65 N

   F_V = 2.99 N

4th August

1. a. 8.0 m^2

   b. 2.0 m^2

   c. 0.50 m^2

   d. 0.13 m^2

2. a. 9.11 x 10^{-31} kg

   b. 6.63 x 10^{-34} J s

   c. 3.00 x 10^8 m s^{-1}

   d. 1.60 x 10^{-19} C

   e. 9.81 N kg^{-1}

   f. 9.81 m s^{-2}

3. 18.3° below horizontal

5th August

1. a. 2.1 m^3

   b. 0.27 m^3

   c. 0.034 m^3

   d. 0.0042 m^3

2. $E_p \propto m$

3. 19 Ω

6th August

1. 0.072 m^3 and 1.6 m^2

2. They should be smooth curves.

3. 32 m

7th August

1. a. 2.3×10^{-3} m^3 8.4×10^{-2} m^2

   b. 1.1×10^{-3} m^3 5.1×10^{-2} m^2

   c. 1.1×10^{21} m^3 5.1×10^{14} m^2

   d. 1.41×10^{27} m^3 6.09×10^{18} m^2

2. a. $T = 1 / f$

   b. $T = W / \theta$

   c. $T = pV / nR$

   d. $T = \sqrt[4]{(P / \sigma A)}$

3. 10 m s^{-1}

8th August

1. a. 1.1 m

   b. 0.45 m

   c. 0.011 m

   d. 0.047 m

2. a. $\omega = P / T$

   b. $\omega = V_{max} / a$

   c. $\omega = \sqrt{(F / mr)}$

   d. $\omega = \sqrt{(2E_k / I)}$

3. 125 Bq

9th August

1. a. 7.2 m^3

   b. 5.7×10^{-5} m^3

   c. 5.2×10^{-6} m^3

2. a. $V = m / \rho$

   b. $V = IR$

   c. $V = NkT / p$

   d. $V = \sqrt{(PR)}$

3. 1100 kPa

10th August

1. y = x + 2

2. a. $v = P / F$

   b. $v = F / BQ$

   c. $v = \sqrt{(Fr / m)}$

   d. $v = \Delta fc / f$

10th August - continued

3. 4.91 m s^{-2}

11th August

1. m = 3 y = 3x - 13

2. a. $r = T / F$

   b. $r = F / 6\pi\eta v$

   c. $r = F / m\omega^2$

   d. $r = v^2 / a$

3. 4000 J

12th August

1. y = -2x +21

2. a. You change this.

   b. This then changes.

   c. You keep these the same.

3. 4.3×10^{14} to 7.5×10^{14} Hz

13th August

1. a. 5.03×10^{-7} m^2

   b. 1.58×10^{-6} m^2

   c. 5.09×10^{-7} m^2

   d. 7.9×10^{-7} m^2

2. y = sin x and y = -sin x

3. 8.0 Ω, 3.6 V and 2.4 V

14th August

1.
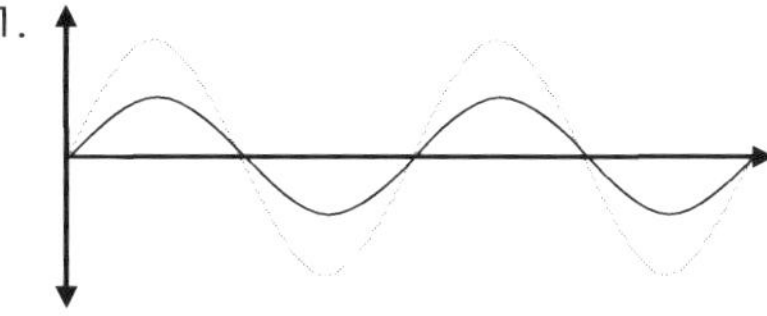

2.
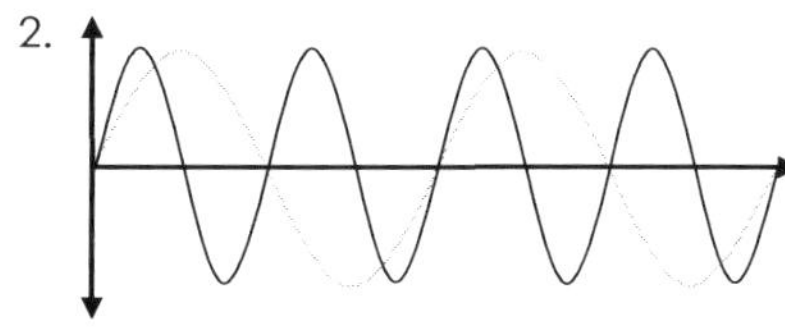

3. 2.5×10^8

15th August

1.
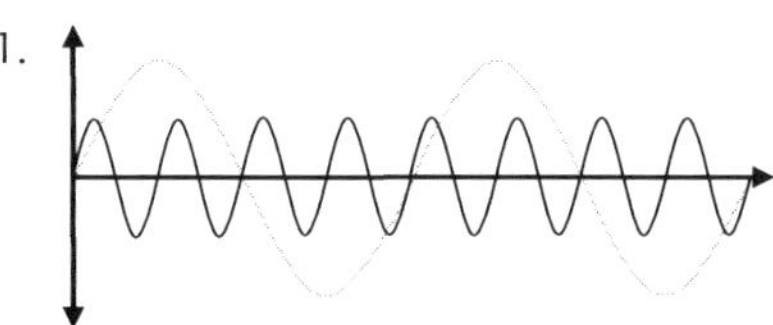

2. a. 6.02×10^{23} mol^{-1}

   b. 8.31 J mol^{-1} K^{-1}

   c. 6.67×10^{-11} N m^2 kg^{-2}

   d. 1.60×10^{-19} C

3. 1.63×10^{-5} m^3

16th August

1. a. 10 > 9

   b. 100 >> 9

   c. 3.7 < 4.1

   d. $660 \times 10^{-9} > 6.5 \times 10^{-7}$

2. a. $\omega_1 = \omega_2 - at$

   b. $\omega_1 = \sqrt{(\omega_2^2 - 2a\theta)}$

   c. $\omega_1 = \sqrt{((\theta/t) - ½at)}$

   d. $\omega_1 = (2\theta/t) - \omega_2$

3. $E_e = ½ke^2$

17th August

1. a. $5.97 \times 10^{24} > 4.87 \times 10^{24}$

   b. $5.97 \times 10^{24} << 1.99 \times 10^{30}$

   c. $5.97 \times 10^{24} << 6 \times 10^{30}$

   d. $9.11 \times 10^{-31} < 1 \times 10^{-30}$

2. a. $\lambda = v / f$

   b. $\lambda = d\sin\theta / n$

   c. $\lambda = ws / D$

   d. $\lambda = D\theta$

3. 130 kg

18th August

1.
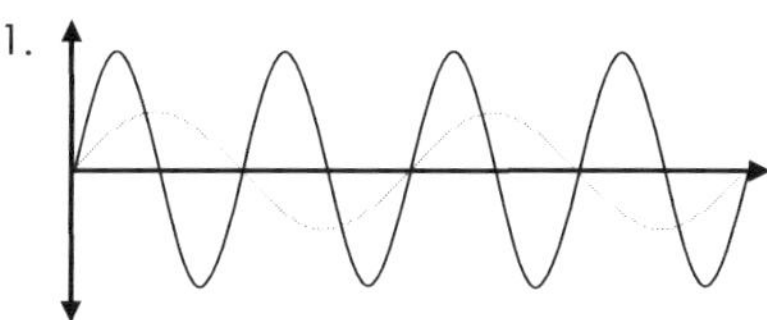

18th August - continued

2. a. $r = kQ / V$

   b. $r = \sqrt{(kQ / E)}$

   c. $r = \sqrt{(kQ_1Q_2 / F)}$

   d. $r = \sqrt{(GMm / F)}$

3. 2.84 kg

19th August

1. A lovely curve.
2. 54˚ 126˚ 54˚
3. a. 1.2 N

   b. 2.2 N

20th August

1. a. $m_{Earth} << m_{Sun}$

   b. $m_p < m_n$

   c. $m_p >> m_e$

   d. Black hole $>> m_{Sun}$

2. 40˚ 70˚ 140˚
3. One part of the wavefront slows down before the other part so it changes direction.

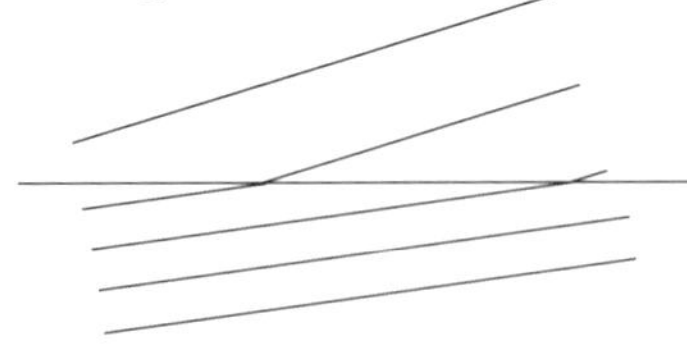

21st August

1. A really lovely curve.
2. a. 180˚

   b. 133˚

3. 5.33 m s^{-1} 0.544 s

22nd August

1. An even lovelier curve!
2. a. B = D

   b. 107˚

3. Two protons and two neutrons ejected.

$$^{A}_{Z}X \rightarrow {}^{A-4}_{Z-2}Y + {}^{4}_{2}\alpha$$

23rd August

1. In a closed system, the total momentum before an event is equal to the total momentum after the event.
2. Reflection occurs when a wave bounces off a surface or boundary. Specular reflection occurs on a smooth surface such that incident parallel rays remain parallel, producing an image. Diffuse reflection occurs on a rough surface, scattering the incident rays such that no image is formed.
3. 10.3 m

24th August

1. The amplitude of a wave is defined as the maximum displacement of a point on a wave away from its undisturbed position.
2. DC is positive to negative but the electrons move from negative to positive.
3. Increasing the collision time for the same change of momentum decreases the size of the force experienced. $F = \Delta p / \Delta t$

25th August

1. In a transverse wave the oscillations are perpendicular to the direction of energy transfer, while in a longitudinal wave they are parallel.
2. Decreasing the volume increases the pressure as there are more collisions per second by the molecules.
3. A neutron changes into a proton, ejecting a high-speed electron.

$$^{A}_{Z}X \rightarrow {}^{A}_{Z+1}Y + {}^{0}_{-1}\beta$$

26th August

1.

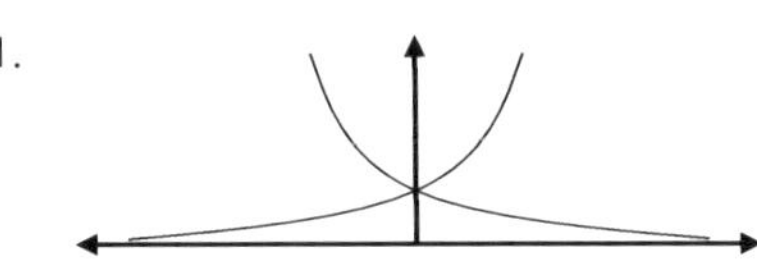

26th August - continued

2. As the temperature decreases the pressure decreases because the molecules are moving slower.
3. 2.07×10^{10} J

27th August

1. The specific heat capacity of a substance is the amount of energy required to raise the temperature of one kilogram of the substance by one degree Celsius (one kelvin).
2. As the temperature increases the volume increases while the gas remains at a constant pressure.
3. Curved line of best fit, ignoring anomaly at 4.0 cm.

28th August

1. a. 0.000

   b. 0.500

   c. 0.707

   d. 0.866

   e. 1.000

2. $F = ma$ and $a = (v-u) / \Delta t$

   $F = (mv - mu) / \Delta t$

   $F = \Delta p / \Delta t$

3. 30˚

29th August

1. a. 1.000

   b. 0.866

   c. 0.707

   d. 0.500

   e. 0.000

2. When they have a constant speed but change direction, for example, objects moving in a circular path.
3. 0.038 A, 0.025 A and 0.063 A

30th August

1. Neat curves.

2.

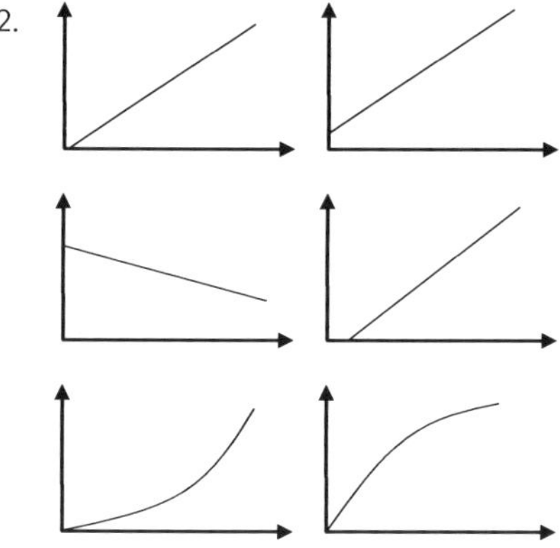

31st August

1. Neat curves.

2.

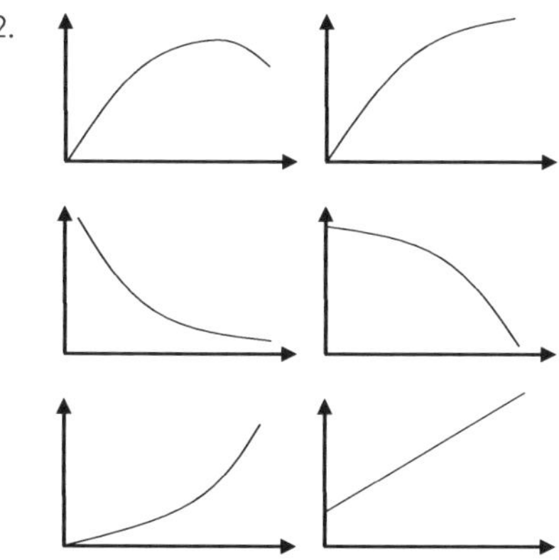

1st September

1. 39.1˚

2. kg m s^{-2}

3. Both can reflect, refract and diffract but only transverse waves can be polarised.

   (T) EM waves, S waves

   (L) Sound, ultrasound, P waves

2nd September

1. 5.7 cm

2. kg m^2 s^{-2}

3. Both can reflect, refract and diffract but mechanical waves have oscillating particles, while electric and magnetic fields oscillate in EM waves.

   (Mech) Sound, seismic waves

   (EM) Radio, visible, gamma

3rd September

1. 0.069 m

2. kg m^2 s^{-3} A^{-1}

3. The force is proportional to the extension provided a spring has not passed the limit of proportionality.

4th September

1. 370 mm

2. kg m^{-1} s^{-2}

3. 58˚

5th September

1. 9.90 cm

2. kg s^{-2} A^{-1}

3. 67˚

6th September

1. a. 9.0×10^{11}

   b. 8.0×10^{12}

   c. 9.0×10^{-9}

   d. 1.2×10^{-1}

2. A quantity with magnitude and direction.

   - Force
   - Velocity
   - Acceleration
   - Displacement
   - Weight
   - Momentum
   - Electric field strength

3. 114˚

7th September

1. A perfect curve.

2. The work done is equal to the force applied multiplied by the distance moved in the direction of the force.

3. 19.2˚

8th September

1. 6760 m

2.

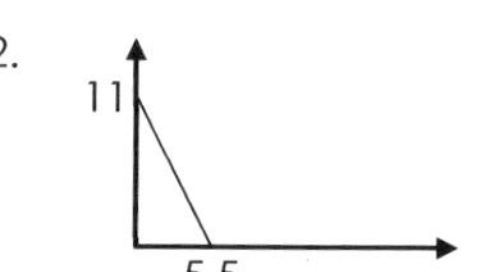

3.

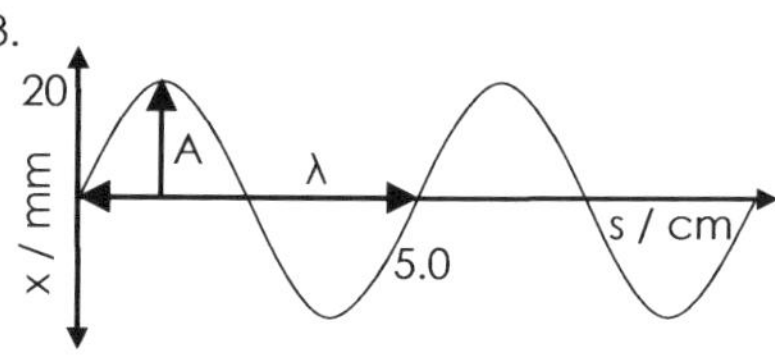

9th September

1. See 13th - 15th July

2. P = Wcosθ

   L = Wsinθ

10th September

1. 1.2

2. a. Mass of an electron

   b. Permittivity of free space

   c. Atomic mass unit

   d. Elementary charge

   e. Planck's constant

   f. One electronvolt

3. P = 91.6

   L = 51.4

11th September

1. 15

2. a. Elastic potential energy

   b. Displacement

   c. Change in momentum

3. $W_{Perpendicular}$ = Wcosθ

   $W_{Parallel}$ = Wsinθ

12th September

1. 7.8

2. a. Resistor

   b. LDR

   c. Fuse

12th September - continued

3. $W_{Perpendicular} = 85.8$ N

   $W_{Parallel} = 47.6$ N

13th September

1. x = AB / (A+B)
2. 22.5
3. $W_{Perpendicular} = 559$ N

   $W_{Parallel} = 437$ N

14th September

1. The current through an ohmic conductor, at constant temperature, is directly proportional to the potential difference across it.
2. a. About 3.5 N at 103°

   b. About 2.9 N at 79°

   c. About 7.7 N at 87°
3. 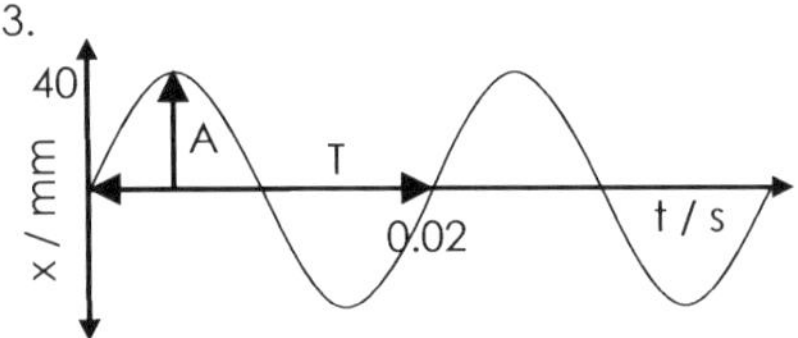

15th September

1. a. 

   b. 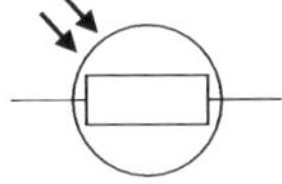

   c. 

   d. 

   e. 
2. a. About 10.5 N at 56°

   b. About 12.2 N at 75°
3. Scalars only have magnitude while vectors have magnitude and direction.

   See 6th September for examples.

16th September

1. a. 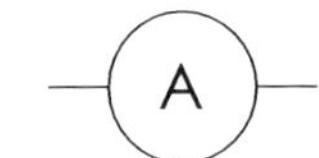

   b. 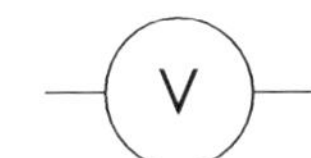

   c. 

   d. M

   e. 
2. Gravitational potential to kinetic to elastic potential, back to kinetic and gravitational potential and so on. Transferring energy to the thermal store throughout.
3. a. About 13 N at 23°

   b. About 15 N at 35°

17th September

1. $p_{FlyingSquirrel} >> p_{Bee}$
2. 78.0 m s^{-1}
3. a. 13.0 N at 22.6°

   b. 14.7 N at 35.3°

18th September

1. a. kg m s^{-1}

   b. Pa

   c. Bq

   d. T
2. 1.1. m
3. About 18.6 kN

19th September

1. Examples include
   - Weight
   - Friction
   - Tension
   - Upthrust/buoyancy

19th September - continued

   - Thrust
   - Lift
   - Normal contact force
   - Drag
   - Weak nuclear
   - Strong nuclear
   - Gravitational
   - Electrostatic
2. The amount of diffraction of a wave is affected by it's wavelength. Monochromatic light has a single wavelength so all the light would diffract by the same value which is easier to measure.
3. 155 780 N at 53.538° from the vertical

20th September

1. a. $V_p = V_s n_p / n_s$

   b. $V_p = V_s I_s / I_p$
2. 2.0 V Step-down
3. 1.7 x 10^4 N

21st September

1. a. 1.84 x 10^{-5} m^2

   b. 9.85 x 10^{-7} m^2

   c. 2.57 x 10^{-8} m^2

   d. 7.74 m^2
2. a. 0.60 A

   b. 0.83 A

   c. 0.65 A
3. a. Displacement (vector) is the distance in a given direction.

   b. Velocity (vector) is the speed in a given direction.

   c. Weight is the force experienced by an object in a gravitational field.

22nd September

1. $R_T = R_1R_2 / (R_1 + R_2)$
2. a. 31 Ω

   b. 7.5 Ω
3. 3.0 m s^{-1}

23rd September

1. a. y = 3x – 1 m = 3 c = -1

   b. y = -3x – 1 m = -3 c = -1

   c. y = 3x + 1 m = 3 c = 1

   d. y = 3x + 9 m = 3 c = 9
2. a. 51 Ω

   b. 5.5 Ω
3. a. x 3 (from 10 Ω to 30 Ω)

   b. ÷ 3 (0.60 A to 0.20 A)

   c. Reduces from 6.0 V to 2.0 V and 4.0 V

24th September

1. a. m s^{-2}

   b. kg m^{-3}

   c. N m^{-1}

   d. N m
2. 3.2 x 10^{-6}
3. a. ÷ 1.5 (from 10 Ω to 6.7 Ω)

   b. x 1.5 (0.60 A to 0.90 A)

   c. Stays at 6.0 V

25th September

1. a. m s^{-2}

   b. J kg^{-1} K^{-1}

   c. J kg^{-1}

   d. N kg^{-1}
2. The structure of metals is a large lattice of positive ions surrounded by a 'sea' of delocalised electrons. Electrons are negatively charged and are free to flow, producing a current when a potential difference is applied.
3. n = 1.5 2.0 x 10^{8} m s^{-1}

26th September

1. You'll be good at this by now.
2. 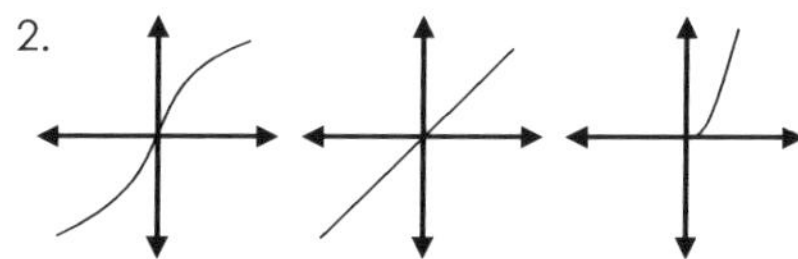
3. 0.75

27th September

1. m = -0.25 y = -0.25x + 3.25
2. 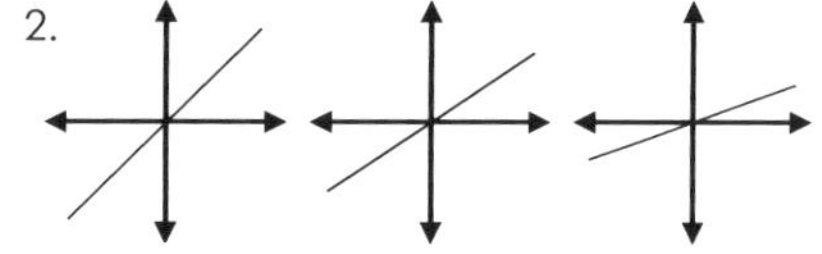
3. 0.75 cm / N

28th September

1. y = -0.1x + 4
2. 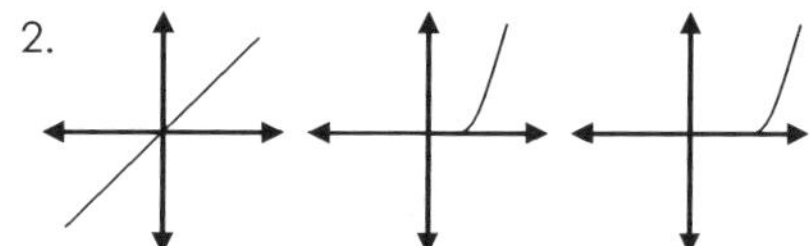
3. -1.6 Ω

29th September

1. a. N

   b. C

   c. Ω

   d. Hz
2. About 780 N at 38° below the horizontal
3. 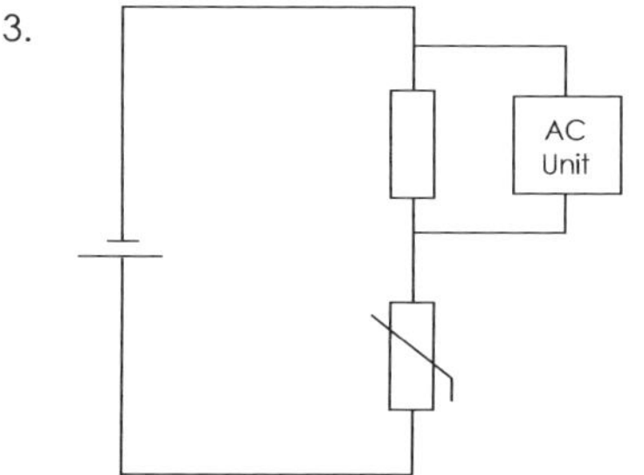

   Potential difference is shared between resistors in series and is the same across resistors in parallel. As temperature increases, the resistance of the thermistor decreases,

29th September - continued

increasing the potential difference across the fixed resistor and hence across the AC unit, turning it on. The AC unit turns off when temperature decreases so that the potential difference across the AC is too low to turn it on.

30th September

1. a. 0.212 m^{2}

   b. 1.4 x 10^{-6} m^{2}

   c. 4.2 m^{2}

   d. 3.10 x 10^{-11} m^{2}
2. kg m^{2} s^{-3}
3. As the light intensity decreases, the resistance of the LDR increases, increasing the potential difference across it as well as the potential difference across the lamp, turning it on. As light intensity increases, the LDR resistance decreases, reducing the potential difference across it and the lamp, so it turns off.

1st October

1. a. 1.1 m

   b. 0.56 m

   c. 1.2 m
2. 20.03 17.34
3. 0.27 A

2nd October

1. a. 9.109 x 10^{-31}

   b. 1.673 x 10^{-27}

   c. 1.675 x 10^{-27}

   d. 6.645 x 10^{-27}

2nd October - continued

2. 17.45 1.20

3. The stationary wave would have antinodes and nodes, points where the wave is at maximum amplitude and zero amplitude respectively. The distance between nodes is equal to half a wavelength. The progressive wave transfers energy along the string.

3rd October

1. a. $d = V / E$

   b. $d = \sqrt{(4A / \pi)}$

   c. $d = n\lambda / \sin\theta$

2. 6.52 2.63

3. n = 1.2

4th October

1. a. $M = -rV_g / G$

   b. $M = -r^2g / G$

   c. $M = -r^2F / Gm$

2. 1.18 0.34

3. -5.67 m s^{-1}

5th October

1. a. 1.50×10^{11} 1 AU

   b. 3.09×10^{16} 1 pc

   c. 9.46×10^{15} 1 ly

2. 46.72 89.40

3. The power dissipated by the wires (whose resistance cannot be ignored) is proportional to the current squared, $P = I^2R$. If the current is reduced by a factor of 10, the power dissipated is reduced by a factor of 100. This makes it very important to transmit electricity at low currents.

6th October

1. a. 6.38×10^6 r_{Earth}

   b. 5.97×10^{24} m_{Earth}

   c. 1.99×10^{30} m_{Sun}

6th October - continued

2. 0.575 s

3. 6.2 N

7th October

1. Mean = 102

   Mode = 104

   Median = 102.5

2. 5.64 m s^{-1}

3. 6.2 N

8th October

1.

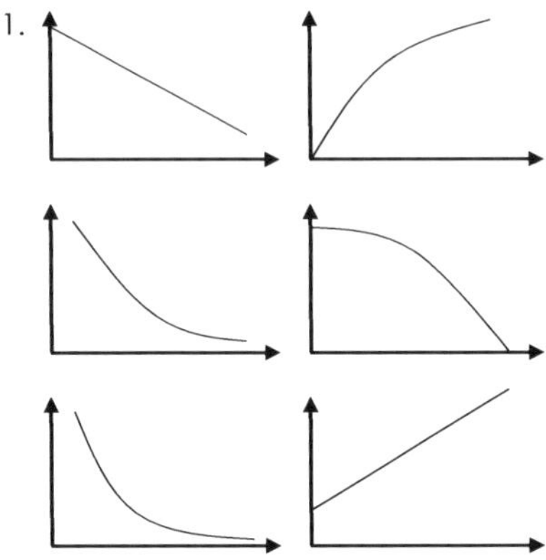

2.

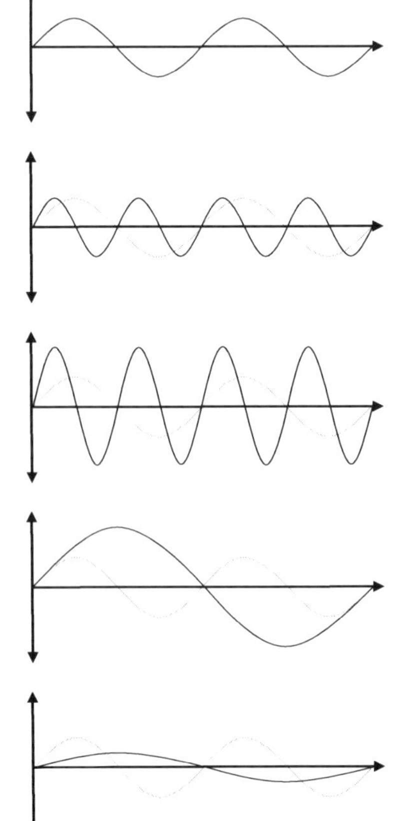

9th October

1. a. 12.6 m^2

   b. 3.14 m^2

   c. 0.785 m^2

   d. 0.196 m^2

2. An accurate result is one that is very close to the true value.

3. Record values of I and V, making sure that the circuit is only briefly switched on while recording data. Plot on an IV graph.

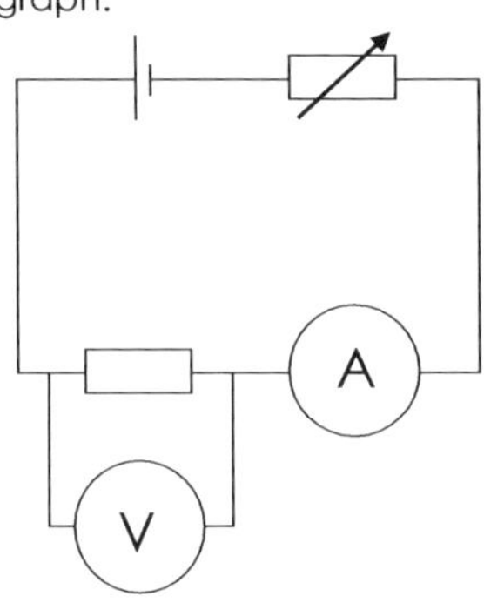

10th October

1. a. 1.08×10^{21} m^3

   b. 1.41×10^{27} m^3

   c. 4.2×10^{-30} m^3

   d. 4.2×10^{-45} m^3

2. Resolution is the smallest scale division on a measuring instrument.

3. a.

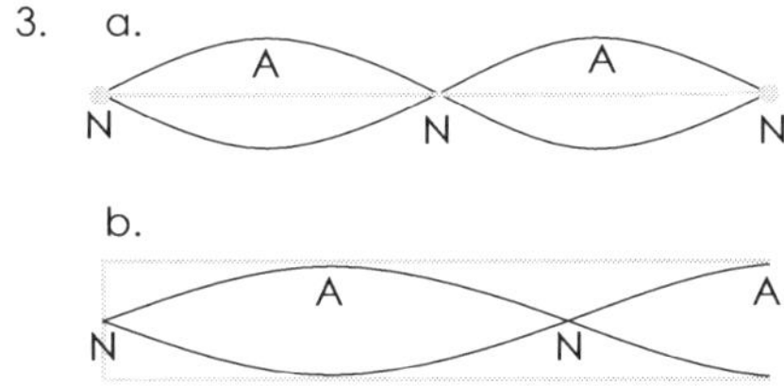

   b.

11th October

1. a. 31.4 m

   b. 3.14×10^{-11} m

   c. 3.14×10^{7} m

   d. 3.14×10^{13} m

   e. 3.14×10^{-6} m

2. 38.20

3. Parallax error is an error in a measurement caused by the viewer's eye not being lined up properly with the object in

11th October - continued

3. question and the measuring instrument. Different angles will give different readings. To reduce parallax error, we need to make sure our eye is looking at the measuring instrument directly in line with the object.

12th October

1. a. 3.14×10^{-13} m

   b. 3.14×10^{-16} m

   c. 3.14×10^{5} m

   d. 3.14 m

   e. 31.40 m

2. 27.81

3. 0.057 Ω^{-1}

13th October

1. 7.7 cm

2. 12.21 29.96

3. 0.044 Ω^{-1}

14th October

1. 8.2 cm

2. 14.03 58.48

3. Increasing the temperature increases the resistance of a wire. The increase in temperature causes the ions within the wire to vibrate more. This reduces the ability for electrons to flow as freely as they collide more often with the vibrating metal lattice, reducing the current flow and increasing resistance.

15th October

1. a. 0.39 0.92

   b. 0.92 0.39

   c. 0.56 0.83

   d. 0.83 0.56

   e. 0.71 0.71

15th October - continued

2. 8.44 1.63

3. a.

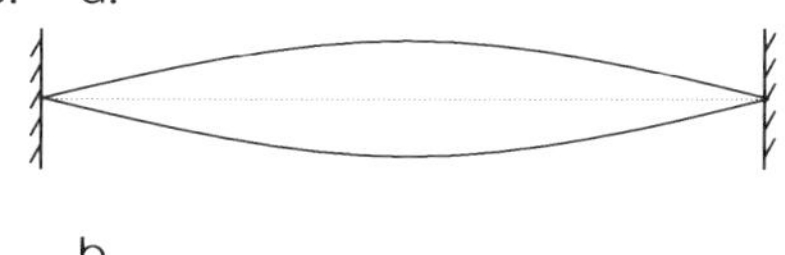

b.

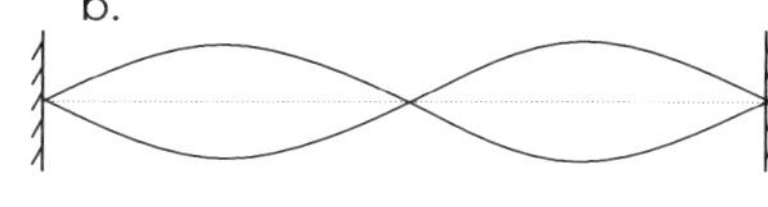

c.

d.

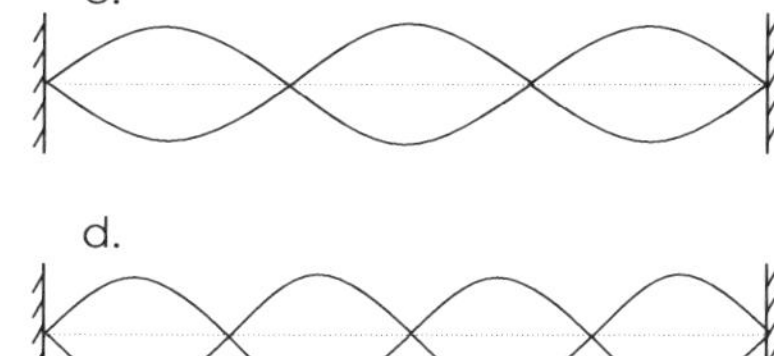

16th October

1. a. 3.60×10^{3} s

   b. 8.64×10^{4} s

   c. 3.16×10^{7} s

2. The current entering a junction is equal to the current leaving the junction, due to the conservation of charge.

3. 9.20 ± 0.05 V

17th October

1. a. 1.0×10^{-6} m^3

   b. 1.0×10^{-9} m^3

   c. 5.68×10^{-4} m^3

   d. 2.24×10^{-2} m^3

2. The sum of potential differences across components in any closed loop in a circuit is equal to the emf supplied, due to conservation of energy.

3. 48 Ω ± 4.4%

18th October

1. a. 1609 m

   b. 6.30×10^{-7} m

   c. 8.33×10^{-16} m

   d. 9.46×10^{15} m

18th October - continued

2. a. $L = (1 / 2f) \sqrt{(T / \mu)}$

   b. $T = 4f^2L^2\mu$

   c. $\mu = T / 4f^2L^2$

3.

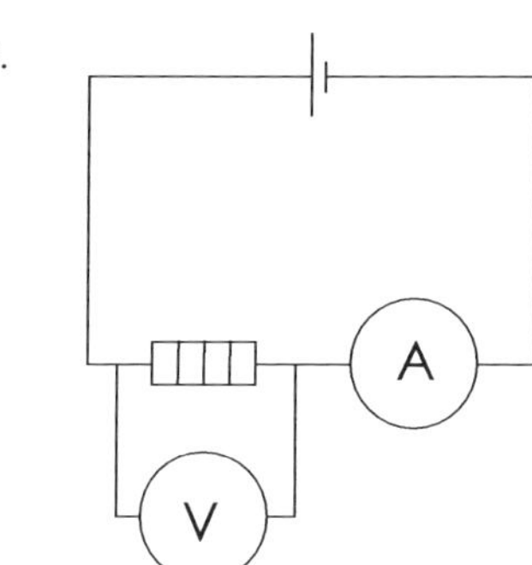

- Insulated beaker
- Heater
- Mass balance
- Thermometer
- Stopwatch
- Power supply
- Ammeter
- Voltmeter

19th October

1. a. 1000 kg

   b. 0.240 kg

   c. 3.560×10^{-3} kg

   d. 93.74 kg

2. A force multiplier will take an input force and multiply it such that the output force is a certain factor greater. In order to not violate the law of conservation of energy, the input force must be moved through a distance that is the same factor greater than the distance the output force is moved through. $W = Fs$. For the same energy transfer, if a force is increased, the distance it is moved through is decreased by the same factor.

3. The moment the skydiver jumps, the only force acting on them is their weight. This causes them to accelerate towards Earth. As they accelerate, their velocity increases therefore the air resistance they experience increases.

19th October - continued

3. The faster they fall, the more air resistance they experience and the smaller the resultant force acting on them, hence the lower their acceleration. The acceleration decreases until the air resistance equals the skydiver's weight, at which point the forces are balanced and the skydiver continues to fall at a constant velocity: terminal velocity.

20th October

1. a. kg m s^{-1}

   b. Ω m

   c. V

   d. kg m^{-1}

2. α m = 6.64 x 10^{-27} kg

   Q = +3.20 x 10^{-19} C

   Low

   β m = 9.11 x 10^{-31} kg

   Q = -1.60 x 10^{-19} C

   Medium

   γ m = 0

   Q = 0

   High

3. The moment the skydiver releases their parachute at high speed, they experience the force of air resistance that is much greater than their weight, so they decelerate (accelerate in the upwards direction). As they slow down, the air resistance decreases until it equals their weight and the forces on the skydiver are balanced. They continue at a slower constant velocity: terminal velocity.

21st October

1. 17°

2. 7.2 N m

3. About -3.0 Ω and 6.6 V

22nd October

1. a. +1.60 x 10^{-19} C

   b. +3.20 x 10^{-19} C

   c. 0 C

   d. +1.07 x 10^{-19} C

2. The centre of mass of an object is the point in space that all of the object's mass can be thought to be concentrated and is the point through which any force being applied will cause linear acceleration but not angular acceleration.

3. Wire: 0 Ω

   Ammeter: 0 Ω

   Voltmeter: ∞ Ω

23rd October

1. a. About 2.6

   b. About -0.50

2. 31.0

24th October

1. Change in momentum or impulse of a force.

2. Progressive waves transfer energy while stationary waves store energy.

3. 8.6 V

25th October

1. a. About 0.63 m s^{-2}

   b. About -0.33 m s^{-2}

2. About 15 m

26th October

1. a. 0.00

   b. 0.58

   c. 1.00

   d. 1.73

   e. ∞

26th October - continued

2. Phase difference is given by the fraction of a complete wavelength between the oscillations of two vibrating particles. This can usually be given in radians at A-Level. Path difference between two waves is the difference in distance travelled, usually to a board or screen where interference has taken place.

3. n = 1.5

27th October

1. a. 0..00 rad

   b. 0.52 rad

   c. 0.79 rad

   d. 1.05 rad

   e. 1.57 rad

2. Draw lines of symmetry on the shape. The centre of mass will lie where the lines of symmetry cross.

3. 4.1 s

28th October

1. a. 0.09 rad

   b. 0.99 rad

   c. 1.43 rad

   d. 3.00 rad

   e. 5.69 rad

2. Suspend the shape from several different points. As the shape settles, the centre of mass will lie directly beneath the point of suspension. Draw vertical lines downwards from each point of suspension. Where these lines cross is where the centre of mass will be.

3. 15 Ω and 8.3 Ω

29th October

1. About 44 m

30th October

1. You've got this!
2. 200 W
3. 4.97 V

31st October

1. 3.1×10^5 m
2. 0.022 m
3. Beyond a certain angle, called the critical angle, all the waves meeting a boundary will reflect back into it. We say that they are totally internally reflected.

   46 °

PHYSICS ONLINE

LEWIS MATHESON

I'm a former **Physics Teacher** and Head of Science, I began making videos to support students back in 2015. Now, I have established websites specialising in GCSE and A Level Physics as well as hugely popular channels on YouTube and TikTok.

Furthermore, I continue to work with many organisations to support teachers, including the Royal Academy of Engineering, Ogden Trust, Institute of Physics, and STEM Learning.

WEBSITES AND SCHOOL SUBSCRIPTIONS

Hundreds of schools now have full access to dedicated websites for both **GCSE** and **A Level Physics** – everyday thousands of students access high-quality videos whenever they need them; these videos include practical experiments, livestreams, worked examples, and regular updates about exams.

Have a look at **ALevelPhysicsOnline.com** to find out more about a **Premium Plan** or **School Subscription** to the website.

Printed in Great Britain
by Amazon